KEEP THE
FAITH

HOW TO STAND STRONG IN A
WORLD TURNED UPSIDE DOWN

DAVID JEREMIAH

W PUBLISHING GROUP

An Imprint of Thomas Nelson

CONTENTS

FOREWORD

It was Barcelona in 1992, and the world was watching. Derek Redmond, a sprinter from Great Britain, was lined up at the starting blocks for the 400-meter Olympic semifinals. Just one more long lap stood between him and the finals—and hopefully his dream of Olympic glory.

Derek had stood in a similar spot four years earlier at the Olympic Games in Seoul, only to tear his Achilles tendon an hour before the first race. The rehab from that injury was long and difficult, but Derek had been at the top of his game in the year before the Games in Barcelona. Then, once the Games began, he had easily won his first two heats to put himself in a great place for the semifinals.

This was his time.

The starter's pistol rang out, and Derek shot from the blocks in a burst of speed. He was running smooth. Running fast. Nearing the halfway point of the race, he was on pace to grab hold of his dream and never let go.

Then, tragedy. Derek popped upward and reached backward toward his thigh. His face contorted into a mask of agony as he collapsed to the ground. His hamstring had torn.

For Derek Redmond, the race was over. His dream was over. His career as an Olympic sprinter was over.

A stretcher team jogged over toward Derek to carry him off the track, but the young man refused. Hobbling back up to his feet, Derek hopped forward on one leg. He made sure to stay in his lane and worked toward the finish line. If he could not win the race, he would at least complete it.

Then, at that bleak moment, something incredible happened. Derek's father, Jim, ran down from the stands and jogged over to join his son. He wrapped an arm around his boy. Held his hand. Derek, overcome with emotion, sobbed on his father's shoulder.

Jim's original goal was to prevent Derek from causing more harm to his leg. "I actually went on the track to try to stop him inflicting further damage to himself," he later told reporters. But Derek had a different goal. "He asked me to get him back in that lane," said Jim, "and I offered him a shoulder to lean on."

Two times, Olympic officials approached Derek and Jim as they limped toward the finish line. They wanted to help move Derek off the track, likely because another race was scheduled to start. Both times, Jim waved the officials away. He was resolute in swatting away any obstacle between his son and his goal. "I saw my [son] having a problem and it was my duty to help."[1]

With his father's help, Derek Redmond crossed the finish line. He finished his race.

I've come across many stories in my decades as a pastor and author, but I can't think of a better illustration of what happens to so many of us over the course of our lives. We start out with dreams. Big dreams. Dreams of success and impact and meaning and purpose. We start the race with high hopes and smiling faces.

Sooner or later, though, life hits back. And life can hit hard.

Maybe you've taken some hits yourself. Maybe, even as you read these pages, you're dealing with something torn. Your health. Your career. Your marriage. Your personal integrity. You're on the ground, watching the other racers sprint ahead, and you're not sure if you can keep going.

If you've been in that place, or if you are in that place even now, remember that your heavenly Father isn't watching impassively from the grandstands of heaven. He has come down. He is close, and His arm is around you. He is lifting you up, and He is ready to help you forward.

The question you have to answer is this: Will you finish the race?

That's the choice you have to make, and it's the same choice faced by the apostle Paul so many years ago. Remember, life hit Paul pretty hard. Actually, it hit him quite a few times—and quite literally. Five times Paul received what the ancient world called "forty stripes minus one," which was a flogging carefully calculated to inflict the maximum amount of pain on a person without killing them. Paul was beaten with rods. He was attacked by mobs. His character was assassinated. He was thrown in prison many times, and he likely spent years in a Roman jail. He was shipwrecked and heartbroken and betrayed.

Yet at the end of it all, he was able to write these words to his spiritual son Timothy: "I have fought the good fight, I have finished the race, I have kept the faith" (2 Timothy 4:7).

How did Paul finish the race? He gave us the answer in that same verse: "I have kept the faith."

That's my goal for you and me as we walk through these pages together—that we would learn what it means to keep the faith even in the most difficult of circumstances and seasons. That we would hold on to our faith as a strong anchor in the storm, and that we would be empowered by that faith when the road seems long and our strength is low.

There will be obstacles of course, and we're going to explore many of them in these pages:

- how to fight fear;
- how to destroy discouragement;
- how to win against worry;
- how to disarm our doubts; and more.

There will be blessings as well. Learning to keep the faith will equip us with wonders including:

- the gift of grace;
- the power of perseverance;
- the role of responsibility;
- the fortitude to handle disruptive moments; and more.

I don't mean to imply the road will be easy or the race will always end in victory. I know from experience that life brings its challenges even for children of God, and I'll share some of my own challenges with you in the pages to come. But as we choose to keep the faith and stay in the race, we will learn how to stand strong and *remain strong* even in a world that seems to be always turning upside down.

Can you feel the Father's strong right arm holding you up? Can you hear Him speaking strength into your heart? Then let's turn the page and discover together what is required of us, and what will be gained by us, when we keep the faith.

—David Jeremiah

CHAPTER 1

FIGHT YOUR FEAR

Ivory Wilderman knew the truth when she saw her doctor's eyes and heard his solemn greeting: "Did you come alone?" The message on his face meant a poor biopsy for Ivory. Minutes later, it was confirmed: the doctors had found breast cancer.

Only moments ago, Ivory's life had never held more promise. At forty-six, she felt the best things in life lining up for her. There was a new job, a new apartment, a new car, and—best of all—a new relationship that could lead to marriage. Life was good; God was blessing. "I wanted to press the Pause button and just enjoy the moment I was in," she says, looking back.

But life has no Pause button. Suddenly Ivory's world began to race out of control in fast-forward. The specialists gave her no more than a 20 percent chance of survival. For the first time, she began to wonder what the experience of death might bring. As she lay awake at night, her fear felt like suffocation. "It was as if a great plastic bag were being fastened around my head," she explains. "There was nothing to do but to call out the name of Jesus."[1]

THE ULTIMATE ENEMY

There's no feeling quite like the icy grip of fear. And it comes in so many varieties.

I've been there; so have you. You've just sampled a story from a friend of our ministry. She was good enough to write us and share her crisis point. (And don't worry: if you'll be patient until the end of the chapter, I'll tell you how her story turned out.)

Hundreds of letters came to our offices at Turning Point after I preached a series on *A Bend in the Road*, inspired by my own fight with cancer. We were showered with amazing accounts of turning points and defining moments. We expected to hear from perhaps eighty of our listeners; I think the final count was eight hundred. And letter after letter spoke of that most deadly of all enemies—*fear*.

That's the terrible thing about the road's bend, isn't it? It's the place where we cannot see what lurks around the corner. Ann Landers, the syndicated advice columnist, was at one time receiving ten thousand letters a month from people with all kinds of problems. Someone asked her if there was one common denominator among all her correspondents. She said that the great overriding theme of all the letters she read was *fear*—fear of nearly everything imaginable until the problem became, for countless readers, a fear of life itself.

Yet fear is simply a part of the fabric of living. God equipped us with it so we would be wise enough to protect ourselves from the unexpected. Fear provides us with sudden bursts of strength and speed just when we need them. It's a basic survival instinct, a good thing—as long as it remains rational. But there's also that brand of fear known as *phobia*. A phobia is what results when fear and reason don't keep in touch.

A woman named Marjorie Goff, for instance, shut her apartment door in 1949. Then, over the next thirty years, she emerged only three times: once for an operation, once to visit her family, and once to buy ice cream for a dying friend. Marjorie suffered from agoraphobia, the fear of open spaces, and the most terrible thing she could imagine was something that might bring pleasure to you or me: an outdoor walk.[2]

I also read about a young truck driver whose route takes him across the Chesapeake Bay Bridge every day. The thought entered his mind that he just might feel compelled to stop the truck, climb out, and leap from the bridge to his death. There was no rational reason to hold such a belief, but that very fear took complete hold of him. He finally asked his wife to handcuff him to the steering wheel so he could be fully assured that his deepest fear wouldn't come true.[3]

That's exactly what fear does when it builds its power over us: it shackles our hands and keeps us from doing the routine things in life—working, playing, living, and serving God. We give in to the slavery of terror.

Chances are, one in ten of those reading this book will suffer from a specific phobia of some type. The other nine will be more like me: they won't be controlled by some irrational fear, but they'll still wrestle with the garden variety of terror—those awful moments when life seems to come undone. Any pastor can tell you stories like the ones at the beginning of this chapter. We sit in hospitals with terrified family members. We hold the trembling hands of those who face uncertain futures. We're often present in the waiting room when the doctor brings the message that dashes hopes, or when the police lieutenant tells us there's no trace of the runaway child. And what about life after the unexpected divorce? The death of a spouse? The loss of a livelihood?

I've had my own moments of overpowering fear. I've stood before huge crowds, afraid to speak. I've sat in football stadiums and watched both of my sons take vicious blows near the neck, then lie motionless on the turf for minutes that seemed like hours. I've sat in the hospital with my daughter Jennifer after she suffered a severe concussion in a soccer game. I doubt any fears are more terrible than those with our children at the center. I've also known the fear of my own impending death, when the doctor brought news of serious disease.

Fear has been described as a small trickle of doubt that flows through the mind until it wears such a great channel that all your thoughts drain into it. Tiny fears, almost unperceived, can build up day by day until we find ourselves paralyzed and unable to function. And there are so many varieties. Craig Massey details six general categories that most of us face: poverty, criticism, loss of love, illness, old age, and death.[4]

WHERE FAITH AND FEAR MEET

But what about Christians? One would think fear to be excess baggage for those who live in the presence of an almighty God. It should be—but it usually doesn't work out that way.

As a matter of fact, fear is one of the biggest obstacles that hinders believers from running the race God has set before us. Fear can keep us curled up on the ground when we should be running free. It can chain our thoughts to the negative circumstances we've encountered in the past, preventing us from relying on and reveling in our hope for the future.

Judging from Scripture, many of God's people were dragged off course because of their fears. The disciples, who had Jesus beside them, seemed constantly fearful—of storms, of crowds, of poverty, of armies, of the loss of their leader. We think immediately of the day Jesus told them to cross over to the other side of the Sea of Galilee. The night closed in like a blanket, a storm came from nowhere, and the disciples found themselves in a fight for their lives as the ship was tossed on the waves. Even when they saw Jesus approaching on the water, they were terrified; they thought He was a ghost (Matthew 14:22–33)! They let fear get the better of them.

The proud Israelite army lived in fear of one man. Of course, the tape measure on that man read nine feet, six inches. Goliath played mercilessly on their fear, taunting them with challenges he knew they wouldn't dare accept. King Saul was ruled by fear—of the giant, then of the boy who slew the giant. David himself wasn't free of fear before the big battle. But he took his slingshot and his five stones and stood tall anyway.

As Mark Twain once said, courage isn't the absence of fear but the *mastery* of it.[5] It's the place where fear and faith meet. In David we have a story of the power of courage—of keeping the faith.

But we also have stories of the power of fear. Perhaps most

notable of all is the one about the delegation of spies who were sent into Canaan. They were commissioned to go on a fact-finding expedition into the unknown territory that lay ahead. This was the promised land—home at last, after generations of slavery in Egypt. It was the land of Abraham, the home-land of their dreams. But they had been away for generations. The land held as much mystery as promise. No doubt about it, Canaan was the bend in the road of the exodus, and the Israelites couldn't see what loomed around that bend. So they assembled in Kadesh Barnea and decided to send out the scouts.

The experience of these men had an impact on Israel that lasted forty years. It cost them years of heartbreak and tragedy. Should they have rushed right in, without the tentative act of sending the spies? We can't say that, since God allowed and encouraged the reconnaissance mission. We can say the men should have come to a different conclusion. The majority failed to see the lay of the land with the perspective God wanted them to have. He didn't ordain the spirit of fear that drove the committee's recommendation.

As we study this narrative carefully, we find key principles about the tyranny of fear and the freedom of faith.

FEAR DISREGARDS GOD'S PLAN

"So we departed from Horeb, and went through all that great and terrible wilderness which you saw on the way to the mountains of the Amorites, as the LORD our God had commanded us. Then we came to Kadesh Barnea. And I said to you, 'You have come to the mountains of the

Amorites, which the LORD our God is giving us. Look, the LORD your God has set the land before you; go up and possess it, as the LORD God of your fathers has spoken to you; do not fear or be discouraged.'"

—Deuteronomy 1:19–21

God's mandate was clear: *Here is your land. Here is My gift to you. Now go grab it!*

With their greatest hopes and dreams laid out before them like beautifully wrapped presents beneath a Christmas tree, the Israelites should have surged forward with joy. They should have claimed all the abundance and fulfillment God wanted them to have. Yet having come so far, having made it through the wilderness with its dusty despair, its hunger and thirst—they couldn't cross the finish line. They had prevailed over Pharaoh's army, over the high tide of the Red Sea, over the challenge of the journey, but they couldn't take a stand against this final obstacle: fear.

You may stand at the threshold of God's greatest promise for you, but you'll never claim His blessings if you let fear dominate your life. He wants so much richness for you in His perfect plan, and only your shortsighted fear can withhold it from you. Listen carefully to the words of Paul on this subject: "God has not given us a spirit of fear, but of power and of love and of a sound mind" (2 Timothy 1:7). Power doesn't shrink back in uncertainty; love isn't conquered; a sound mind doesn't deal in irrational speculation. God has a rich territory, a promised land with your name on it, and He wants you to charge toward it with a cry of victory, not a wail of fear.

The Bible even tells you what that cry of victory should

sound like: "You did not receive the spirit of bondage again to fear, but you received the Spirit of adoption by whom we cry out, 'Abba, Father'" (Romans 8:15). Call out His name. This verse assures us we can claim the intimacy with Him of a small child calling out to their father. He has adopted us as His own, and we have all the rights of the children of the King. We don't have to face anything alone.

The truth is, God has a plan for your life. He has a race for you to run, and you can sprint toward the finish line with joyful assurance. Fear disregards that opportunity and holds us back. Have you ever seen a timid, cowering prince? Stop living as a helpless street orphan when you bear the credentials of the King.

FEAR DISTORTS GOD'S PURPOSES

Fear does one very predictable thing: it distorts our view. Fear robs us of our perspective. Listen to Moses as he summarized the attitudes of his people:

> "And you complained in your tents, and said, 'Because the LORD hates us, He has brought us out of the land of Egypt to deliver us into the hand of the Amorites, to destroy us. Where can we go up? Our brethren have discouraged our hearts, saying, "The people are greater and taller than we; the cities are great and fortified up to heaven; moreover we have seen the sons of the Anakim there."'"
> —Deuteronomy 1:27–28

Fear brings out our worst. It ushers in complaining, distrust, finger-pointing, and despair. You can see them all in these verses. God had provided victory over the Egyptian oppressors. He had given deliverance through the wilderness. He had offered a new plan for living through the commandments on Mount Sinai. And now He was offering real estate—the gift of a new land for building a nation. But in fear, the people were cowering in their tents to gripe about God's intentions. "God brought us all this way just to deliver us to the Amorites."

Fear does that to us, doesn't it? When you talk to a terrified friend or family member, you find yourself wanting to say, "But that's silly!" For it's easy for us to see the irrationality and absence of perspective of other people ruled by fear. The spies brought back a distorted picture, and they infected the whole nation with it. "There are giants in the land! Anakim!" That word held terror for the Israelites. It was synonymous with monstrous, marauding giants. But of course, while they did see a giant or two, the only formidable one was the giant inside their heads—and that giant's name was Fear.

It's worth reading the parallel account in Numbers 13:32–33, where we find the fears of the spies painted in even darker tones. The land "devours its inhabitants," they said. "We were like grasshoppers in our own sight, and so we were in their sight."

Fear is an army of giants, for it multiplies one into many. Fear also makes us grasshoppers in our own eyes. We lose sight of the promise that we can do all things through Him who strengthens us. We lose the ability to see anything in its true perspective. Fear, not the object of the fear, devours its inhabitants.

In the imaginations of the spies there were massive, fortified cities teeming with giants. So great was their distorted perspective that they even made an evil giant out of God. "Why, He brought us all this way to make us food for the heathen," they said. I defy anyone to find any logic at all behind their conclusion. But haven't we all said such a thing? "God is out to get me! He's brought me all this way to make me miserable!" The greater the fear, the weaker our reasoning.

Fear distorts our perception of God's purposes. It shows life through a fun-house mirror—without the fun.

FEAR DISCOURAGES GOD'S PEOPLE

The third effect of fear is that it reaches its tendrils out to everyone around us. Discouragement is contagious. When you give in to your fears, you make the world around you an environment of discouragement. That word, *discourage*, means to take away courage. Fear causes us to drain away the vitality of people we care for.

This is a devastating principle, isn't it? Fear is catching; eventually it breeds hysteria. Ten men out of twelve came back with what the Bible calls a "bad report," and those ten infected an entire nation—not just for a week or a month but for a generation. The golden hopes and dreams of the Israelites—for land, for security, for a new beginning—were ruined for forty years because of the fear of ten men. When the spies returned from their journey, they brought a giant back with them, one much more terrible than the mere men they had seen. This giant of Fear prowled through their camp and devoured the faith and courage of a nation.

If you don't think fear is contagious, imagine standing in

the hallway at work and calling out one word: "Fire!" You'd be successful in changing the moods and plans of hundreds of people in an instant. You would also endanger everyone around you. Fear is more infectious than any disease you can name. It roams the landscape and discourages God's people.

FEAR DISBELIEVES GOD'S PROMISES

"Then I said to you, 'Do not be terrified, or afraid of them. The LORD your God, who goes before you, He will fight for you, according to all He did for you in Egypt before your eyes, and in the wilderness where you saw how the LORD your God carried you, as a man carries his son, in all the way that you went until you came to this place.' Yet, for all that, you did not believe the LORD your God, who went in the way before you to search out a place for you to pitch your tents, to show you the way you should go, in the fire by night and in the cloud by day."

—Deuteronomy 1:29–33

The challenge before the Israelites wasn't something that came out of nowhere and demanded that they trust some mysterious, untested providence. This was the invitation of the God who had gone with them throughout their journey. This was the loving Father who had remained so steadfast by their sides and who had provided every need. This was One worthy of the same trust a tiny child would place in his loving parents—and so much more worthy.

Indeed, God called them the *children* of Israel, and the Bible tells us that He carried them along as you would carry an infant. He watched over them as you would guard your newborn baby. He led their steps, provided their food, saw to their protection, and did everything possible to nurture a loving and fully trusting relationship. The point of the wilderness experience was for the people to bond with their Father. After generations of slavery under their tyrannical masters in Egypt, God wanted His children to learn something of the wonderful journey that transpires when we follow Him.

He wanted to show them the joy of keeping the faith!

But learning always involves testing. And that's what happened when the spies were appointed—the people were given a test to reveal whether they really trusted God.

The children of Israel had everything they needed to pass this test. But I believe they experienced a principle that seems more true and clear to me with every passing day. It seems to me that every defining moment of faith is just like starting over. Yes, we have the past to build on; just like the Israelites, we *should* be able to look back and say, "God has brought us this far; He will bring us home." Memory and experience should empower us. But we struggle to do that very thing; the moment's crisis seems to magnify itself. The rearview mirror should give us perspective, but we don't look at the mirror at all—our eyes are frozen by what's in the headlights.

The Israelites certainly are a testimony to that. There were giants in their headlights. And those giants seemed so fantastically massive that they blocked out what God had done in the past, what He was doing in the present, and His Word on the future.

Fear disbelieves God's promises.

FEAR DISOBEYS GOD'S PRINCIPLES

Deuteronomy 1:26 says, "Nevertheless you would not go up, but rebelled against the command of the LORD your God." It's a harsh truth but an insistent one: fear is disobedience, plain and simple. How can fear be anything other than disobedience to God, when He has given us everything we need to walk in faith?

There's a little phrase in the Bible—such a simple phrase, and one that God sees fit to repeat so often, all throughout the Scriptures. It goes like this: *fear not*. That phrase, if you'll notice, is stated in the imperative tense—which simply means it is a command. How many times must God command us not to fear? "Therefore, to him who knows to do good and does not do it, to him it is sin" (James 4:17). The next time you find yourself overcome by fear, remember—along with all of God's other promises and assurances—that to dwell in fear is to live in sin.

But doesn't that seem a bit strict and inflexible? Your first response might be, "I can't help it! I don't want to be fearful, but it's out of my control." And if that's how you feel, you've forgotten that God has given us everything we need to deal with fear. He has provided us with principles of faith that help us live courageously.

When all is said and done, any alternative to His way boils down to simple disobedience—something that is always costly. For the nation of Israel, it meant a lost generation. The adult group of that time was forbidden from finding their journey's end for forty years. They were sentenced to a restless, nomadic life of wandering homeless in the desert, waiting for the last of that forsaken group to finally die. Only two of them were permitted entry into Canaan: Joshua and Caleb, who had stood firm in their faith. Courage earned them their home, yet they, too, wandered along the borders during those forty years, attending the funerals of their friends. When the last body was laid to rest, the nation could finally claim its true home.

FACING THE GIANT OF FEAR

God longs for you and me to simply accept the gifts from His hand. He has a more wonderful and fulfilling home for someone, a life partner for someone else, a thrilling new opportunity for ministry or career direction for still someone else. But fear cuts us off from accepting these prizes. I often counsel friends who are feeling God's tug at their hearts. He has something special for them to do, and they can look forward to blessings in abundance if only they'll be obedient and trusting.

They want to accept the call—but fear holds them back, always some new fear. *What if I'm making the wrong decision? What if this isn't the right partner for me? What if my business venture fails? What if I get homesick on the mission field? What if, what if?* Somehow they can't hold to a simple assurance of God's trustworthy and loving nature. It doesn't seem to register that He never calls His children only to desert them. (*Would He lead us this far only to deliver us into the hands of the Amorites?*)

I've seen where this failure of trust leads—right to the doorstep of heartbreak. Those who shrink back from accepting God's gift condemn themselves to lives of fitful, restless wandering through the wildernesses of their jobs and their communities and their broken dreams. Fields of milk and honey stood in wait, but they settled for less.

My question to you is: Isn't that kind of disappointment in life far more to be feared than the risk of taking God at His word? Of course it is. The question, then, is what to do about it.

How can we face our fears? How can we hold on to faith?

CONFRONT YOUR FEAR HONESTLY

You may long for your fear to simply vanish or wear off, but it isn't going anywhere—not on its own. If you want to defeat it, you must be like David: gather up your stones and advance boldly!

First, understand what is at the root of your fears. Often people have come to me and said, "I don't know what I'm afraid of; I just have a spirit of fear." Is that your experience? Look a little deeper and get a specific reading on what is causing your feelings. Ask God to search your heart for you. He knows where the problem lies, but you need to let Him show you. Otherwise, you're going to simply run away—and like Jonah, you'll find that you can run, but you can't hide.

I read the remarkable story of a family from Canada. These people were convinced a world war was looming, and they were terrified. They decided to run away, hoping to find some corner of the planet where they would be free and clear from the fighting. In the spring of 1992, they relocated to a quiet little spot known as the Falkland Islands, an obscure piece of British real estate. The family relaxed and enjoyed five days of tranquility before the Argentinians invaded their backyard and began the famous Falklands War.[6]

There's nowhere to run. Better to take a stand and face the truth of the fear. What is it that really concerns you? Why?

CONFESS YOUR FEAR AS SIN

We've already seen that fear boils down to disobedience. God says, "Fear not." But we do fear. We are, therefore, in sin. The only thing to do is to come to God for honest confession.

Again, some may feel this stance is harsh or unrealistic. After all, we can't help what we feel, can we? Up to a point, that's very true. Emotions come to us on their own. But it's also true that we have the power to act on our feelings—or not. We can choose by will to obey God's voice. We can make it our daily, serious intention to fill our lives and thoughts and plans with His Word and His truth. "I sought the LORD, and He heard me, and delivered me from all my fears" (Psalm 34:4). To walk with God is to walk fearlessly.

So we identify the fear, then we confess it. As we bring our fear before God and own up to it, we do one other thing. We repent. That means to disavow the sin completely, to turn and walk the other way. Then we can look toward the steps that lead us to victory over our fears.

CLAIM GOD'S PROMISES OF PROTECTION

The next step is all about taking advantage of wonderful, untapped resources. Most people simply don't realize the treasure that lies at their fingertips. The Bible is filled with practical promises. Any one of them, if we choose to take hold of it, leads to liberation from some tough problem of life.

If I were a person with a fearful spirit, I'd go to the store and buy a package of three-by-five index cards. Then I would turn to certain verses in my Bible and copy them onto the cards. I'd place one on the visor of my car. I'd tape one to the wall of my bathroom. One would be slid under the glass of my desk. Another would find a home in my wallet, and I might even tape one to the television remote! I'd type the text in colorful letters on my computer screen so that I'd see it there whenever I walk through the room. I would then be well prepared for the first tingle of oppression from a spirit of fear. I could reach for that Bible verse, read it out loud, repeat it again, and ask God to demonstrate its truth in the battlefield of my heart and spirit.

Are you interested in tapping into that wealth of promises? I'll give you several, and I suggest you read them out loud and reflect on their vital significance for you.

- Deuteronomy 31:6: "Be strong and of good courage, do not fear nor be afraid of them; for the LORD your God, He is the One who goes with you. He will not leave you nor forsake you."
- Psalm 27:1: "The LORD is my light and my salvation; whom shall I fear? The LORD is the strength of my life; of whom shall I be afraid?"
- Psalm 118:6: "The LORD is on my side; I will not fear. What can man do to me?"
- Proverbs 3:25–26: "Do not be afraid of sudden terror, nor of trouble from the wicked when it comes; for the LORD will be your confidence, and will keep your foot from being caught."

- Proverbs 29:25: "The fear of man brings a snare, but whoever trusts in the Lord shall be safe."

The next one is a personal favorite. I suggest you put a big star beside it:

"Fear not, for I am with you; be not dismayed, for I am your God. I will strengthen you, yes, I will help you, I will uphold you with My righteous right hand."

—Isaiah 41:10

Those verses are the best fear insurance you can invest in. Memorize them. Write them out or print them on cards, and place them in locations where you might be attacked. Let the Word of God fortify your spirit.

And of course, those verses are only the beginning. Read through God's Word, and you'll find so many more assurances for times of fear. The inspired writers knew what it was like to be afraid in the ancient world; they had fears we can't even imagine. Peter and Paul had to face fear. Jesus prayed in Gethsemane, knowing exactly what lay ahead for Him in the hours to come. They all found their strength in God, and you can benefit richly from their spiritual wisdom. Look up *fear* in your Bible's concordance, and then look up *afraid*.

Take in all these passages, soak in their power, and the next time the devil comes to get a response out of you, you'll be ready. Pull five verses from the living water just like five smooth stones in David's pouch, and let them fly! Don't worry about that fearsome giant; the bigger they come, the harder they fall.

The next step may sound so simple, so basic, that you may shrug it aside. I hope you won't do that!

CULTIVATE A CLOSER RELATIONSHIP WITH GOD

Yes, you can confront your fears by drawing near to God. What better way to keep the faith than to connect with Him who is altogether faithful?

Think back to those spies who entered Canaan. Think about the two dissenters in that group. They went on the same trip, saw the same walled cities and the same giants, and they brought back a minority opinion. Joshua and Caleb listened patiently to all the worst-case scenarios and calmly said, "We can do this."

As I've read this narrative over the years, I've always felt that the difference between the ten and the two was that they used different yardsticks. The negative group measured the giants by their own stature, while Joshua and Caleb measured them by God's stature. These two were the only ones who finally measured up to the privilege of entering the promised land. The others fell short.

What made the difference for Joshua and Caleb? The Scriptures state it clearly.

In Numbers 32:12 we read: "For they have wholly followed the LORD." You'll find the same message in Deuteronomy 1:36 and Joshua 14:9. Joshua and Caleb were simply different creatures from the rest. The Bible makes it clear that they were absolutely filled with the Spirit of God, and they walked with Him in every way. It caused them to think differently, act differently, decide differently. And when the time of crisis came—the time when we find out what people are made of—Joshua and Caleb were living proof of what it means to have godly courage. These two looked at a land that "devoured its inhabitants" and said, "This is God's will for us. Let's do it!"

Your fear level is ultimately a referendum on the closeness of your friendship with God. It's a spiritual yardstick. Do you see things in human dimensions or godly ones? After you spend time with your Creator, you're simply incapable of shrinking in fear at the appearance of every human anxiety. You've seen His power. You've seen His love and faithfulness. You've seen that His purposes are the best for us. If you have "the fear of God," as we used to say, you won't fear the things of this world. If you don't have the fear of God, then everything else is to be feared.

There's one other verse that in my judgment is the essential New Testament verse on this subject. Think about it carefully; I'd suggest memorizing it: "There is no fear in love; but perfect love casts out fear, because fear involves torment. But he who fears has not been made perfect in love" (1 John 4:18).

The opposite of fear, you see, is not courage. It's not trust. The opposite of fear is *love*. This verse captures that beautiful and powerful truth. As we've already seen near the beginning of this chapter, "God has not given us a spirit of fear, but of power and of love and of a sound mind" (2 Timothy 1:7). There it is again—fear versus love. I think parents understand this principle, for they know that little children often wake up in the dark of night. And they're afraid of the darkness. I experienced it with our grandson David Todd. Sometimes when he would visit, he would wake up in that unfamiliar bedroom in the middle of the night and begin to cry. It wasn't just any kind of crying, but an "I'm afraid" kind of crying. You parents know what I mean.

So what would we do? I doubt any of us would have rushed into the room and said, "Come on, David—be courageous!" No, you and I are much more tender than that. We lifted the little boy in our arms, nestled him tightly to us, and spoke softly with assurance. We told him we loved him and that everything would be all right. We helped him realize he was in a safe place and that, in spite of the darkness, we were very near as he slept and would always protect him. And we poured in all the love we could until the fear was cast out and our little grandchild slept in peace. That's what God does for us when we call on Him.

Harry Ironside, a great preacher from years ago, told the story of playing a game called Bears with his young son. The grown-up would be the bear, and he'd chase the boy all over the house. But one day the game got a bit too intense. The boy was cornered by the "bear," and he suddenly became truly frightened—it wasn't a game anymore. He hid his face, trembling, and then turned around quickly and threw himself into his father's arms with the words, "I'm not afraid of you! You're my daddy!"

Our Father wants us to leap into His arms in just that way whenever we're afraid. He wants us to realize who He really is and that we need never fear. And the key to that assurance is love, the opposite of fear. To experience in full the love of God is to feel the deepest security in heart, soul, mind, and strength. It is to understand, down to the depth of our being, that God loves us so much He will always fold us in His arms; that He'll always be near, even when it's dark; that He is our

Daddy and that we need not be afraid. And we realize all of this as His incomprehensible love washes through us and cleanses us from fear and anger and selfishness. Then and only then do we find ourselves capable of returning love—for remember, "We love Him because He first loved us" (1 John 4:19).

And that's when it happens: love begins to dispel fear. Yes, we'll be visited by fears again because they're part of living. But they'll never have the same hold on us. They'll be the reasonable fears of touching the hot stove or crossing the busy street. The irrational, controlling fears will not be allowed to dominate the heart, for the heart is home to the Holy Spirit now. He will not allow it. As a matter of fact, we won't have time to nurture some deep fear and build it up to become a giant, because the Spirit will see that our hands are active in ministry. We'll be too busy running the race to worry about fear!

It's an amazing principle: the more you reach out to other people with needs, the smaller your fears become. Again, this is love casting out fear.

This is one more good reason to become active in ministry. Be an encourager. Be an ambassador of the love of God. I know of no better prescription for misery of any kind. As you can see, there's nothing trite about my advising you to cultivate a closer relationship with God. That's the ultimate fear strategy. Children who are afraid call on their parents. It's no different for adults who are afraid, but the Parent whose name we call is so much more powerful, so much more loving, so much more responsive. If your life is filled with anxiety and irrational fears, draw near to God, starting today. Increase your time in His Word. Devote more time to prayer, and keep a prayer journal of how He comforts you in times of fear.

My final point calls on you to be certain you're able to draw near to Him.

COMMIT YOUR LIFE TO JESUS CHRIST

There is one ultimate fear every human being must face—one fear that stands taller than all the others. The ultimate giant is Death itself.

The fear of death causes people to do strange things. I once knew a man who kept a canister of oxygen in every room in his home. His cars had those little tanks. The bathrooms, the bedrooms, the kitchen, garage—everywhere there were oxygen canisters. One day, as I visited with him, I asked him the meaning of this obsession. He explained, "Well, I have a little bit of a heart problem. I'm afraid that one of these days I might have a heart attack, and I won't be able to get the oxygen I need—then I'll die."

He concluded, "I'll do everything in my power to hedge my bet." And so, to smother his life in security, he'd made it into a life that was all about oxygen canisters.

Caution is a good thing; phobias are unhealthy. When the appointed day arrives and God calls you home, all the oxygen canisters in the world will not buy you another second of life. The real question is, Are you desperate for another second, another hour, another day? If so, why does death hold so much terror for you? Are you so eager to avoid the beautiful gates of heaven and the open arms of God?

I know now that I'm not afraid of death. I can say this because I've been right out to the edge of mortality, looked death in the face, and discovered that I'm not afraid. I'm willing to move on to my next destination—though I'm not eager to get a head start. I happen to love life. I'm devoted to my ministry and my family, and I have no desire to die. But it's a wonderful thing to come to a sense of peace about the finality of this life. It's good to be able to say, "I'm not afraid to die."

Paul understood that it's a win-win situation for God's people. He wrote, "For to me, to live is Christ, and to die is gain" (Philippians 1:21). We can stay on earth and experience the joy of Christ, or we can move on to the next life and occupy those mansions He's gone to prepare. Either way, we've got it made. Why fear for things in this life? Why fear the doorway that leads to the next one?

Yet you and I both know people who move through this life wearing the shackles of a lifelong fear of death. The chains hold them back from any enjoyment or fulfillment in life. But there's an interesting passage in Hebrews that tells us how we ought to think about death:

> Inasmuch then as the children have partaken of flesh and blood, He Himself likewise shared in the same, that through death He might destroy him who had the power of death, that is, the devil, and release those who through fear of death were all their lifetime subject to bondage.
>
> —2:14–15

There it is in a nutshell—the most important truth of history. Death had dominion over this world. All people had to live in its tyranny, and life was dominated by death. Then God came into the world in the guise of human flesh, in order to share everything we experience. He stretched out His arms on that great wooden cross, and He gave Himself up. As the sky darkened and the earth shook and history turned upside down, Jesus hung between heaven and earth, bridging the ultimate gulf that could not be closed in any other way.

That changed everything. He brought eternity back to you and me, and He brought us home again to God. The power of death was totally broken. Death has no power at all outside of the lies and distortions of the deceiver. The devil wants you to believe that death is still a giant. He wants you to believe your sins still give death the final word and that you must therefore live in terror. But the truth is that Jesus paid the debt. Your sins will not be held against you now if you'll accept the gift that Jesus purchased with His life.

We can rest in that assurance and find liberation from fear. We can trust God, as Ivory Wilderman did. She endured surgery, chemotherapy, and radiation. No matter what happened, she told herself, God would be there. Through the long nights of uncertainty she called out God's name, sought Him through the Scriptures, and clung to her faith with desperation. God drew near. "The victory came," she said, "as I took my thoughts captive, prayed, read the Bible, recalled verses I'd memorized, and sang potent praise songs. With each conquest, the fearful thoughts grew weaker." Today she is married, a mother (miraculously after the treatments), and the founder of a successful support group for cancer victims. "God is victorious!" she says with joy.

Yes, God is victorious. So are we, when we take the counsel of God's Word. Fear not! Keep the faith! There are giants in the land, but next to our Lord they're little more than grasshoppers.

CHAPTER 2

DESTROY YOUR DISCOURAGEMENT

It was clear to Doretha that her husband drank too much. But what could she do about it? Whenever she confronted him about his problem, he flew into a rage—which only made the drinking worse. Since there didn't seem to be any viable options, Doretha simply tried to ignore the problem and concentrate on raising their son. She focused everything on motherhood.

Soon, that wouldn't be an option either.

One autumn evening in 1995, Doretha's husband was foolishly handling his gun while he was under the influence of alcohol. His hands slipped, the gun went off, and a bullet took the life of their son.

With her husband in jail, Doretha was left to the silence

and despair of an empty house. She no longer had any real desire to live, but she was also afraid to die. A lifetime ago, at age thirteen, she had joined a church, but issues of life and death and eternity were all equal mysteries to her now.

Doretha remembers climbing into her car late at night and driving for hours in the hope that maybe she'd drift off to sleep and quickly be delivered from her waking nightmare. But something protected her every time. In the daylight, she began visiting churches. It was good medicine at the time, but the effects wore off when she left the sanctuary and reentered the roaring silence of her home.

What exactly are the limits to human tolerance? What are the units of measurement for pain and discouragement, and how does your discouragement threshold differ from mine?

I'm not sure about the answer to those questions, but the human spirit can be an amazing thing. Take the case of Lawrence Hanratty, who was named the "Unluckiest Man in New York City." This poor fellow, profiled in the *Los Angeles Times*, was nearly electrocuted to death in a construction site accident in 1984. For weeks he lay in a coma, with his lawyers fighting for his disability claim—until one of them was disbarred and two of them died. Hanratty's wife then ran off with her lawyer.

Hanratty later lost his car in a terrible crash. After the police had left the scene of the accident, criminals came along and robbed him. Then an insurance company fought to cut off his workers' compensation benefits, and his landlord tried to evict him. He suffered from depression and agoraphobia.

He required a canister of oxygen for breathing and took forty-two pills per day for his heart and liver ailments.

Talk about feeling like the world has turned upside down!

Still, all was not lost. A city councilman took up his cause. Neighbors began to rally around him. Incredibly, Lawrence Hanratty summed up his life this way: "There's always hope."[1]

LOSING HEART

Would you be able to talk about hope after a string of unthinkable calamities? Have you accentuated the positive and eliminated the negative during the low points of your life?

We know those words are true—*there's always hope*—but sometimes it's hard to believe them. All of us suffer through bouts of discouragement. The dictionary defines *discourage* as "to deprive of courage, to deter, to dishearten, to hinder." All those *D* words—and you can throw in *doom, depression, defeat, despair*. The mind dwells on them when life has us pinned down.

The New Testament uses three Greek words to carry the idea of being disheartened, dispirited, or discouraged. We often translate them as "to faint" or "to lose heart." For example, Paul warned us to take special care not to become the source of discouragement for our children: "Fathers, do not provoke your children, lest they become *discouraged*" (Colossians 3:21, emphasis added). And in 2 Corinthians 4:1, he spoke to those who may become disheartened in ministry: "Therefore, since we have this ministry, as we have received mercy, we do not lose heart." Later in that chapter, he encouraged us not to become discouraged as the "outward man" deteriorates because what's inside us is being renewed daily (v. 16).

And we shouldn't be discouraged by the plight of our loved ones, for in Ephesians 3:13, Paul wrote, "Do not lose heart at my tribulations for you."

Jesus brought up the subject of discouragement in the context of prayer. "He spoke a parable to them," Luke 18:1 tells us, "that men always ought to pray and not lose heart." There's so much truth in that verse. We must live and breathe and take up residence in prayer, or we're sure to faint, to grow weary, to lose heart. It takes diligent faith to live above discouragement.

Lest you think this is purely a personal issue, remember that entire nations can run out of hope. It happened during the darkest days of Israel and Judah, when the invaders rolled in. The Babylonians destroyed the holy city of Jerusalem, looting its glories and carrying away its people to enslavement in a distant land. It seemed that God's chosen people had lost it all—their land, their pride, their very identity as a nation set apart for a special destiny, for now God's children were dispersed across the nations. These were the darkest times, days of lamentation and weeping and silence.

But as Lawrence Hanratty said, there's always hope. A ruler named Cyrus the Persian came to power, and he gave permission for Jewish exiles to begin the homeward journey. In the time of the first return and the rebuilding of the temple, we think of two biblical heroes: a priest named Ezra and an administrator named Nehemiah. Each has a book of his own in our Bible, but there was a time when their two accounts were combined in one longer book.

Ezra was the priest to broken hearts, and Nehemiah was the rebuilder of broken dreams. The second one offers a liberating lesson for us about the renovation of hope from the rubble of discouragement. Let's explore that story in greater detail as a powerful example of what it means to stand strong even in the face of discouragement.

BUILDING BLOCKS

The fourth chapter of Nehemiah's book puts us in the middle of exciting times. Nehemiah, the gifted organizer, has arrived in a chaotic situation, but he has galvanized a community and jump-started the rebuilding operation. With the walls lying in ruins, the people of Israel haven't had the luxury of peaceful sleep. Raiders from the outlying provinces have been able to attack by night and keep the Israelite settlers discouraged and fearful. This has been done very deliberately. The threat of a Hebrew revival is an unwelcome one to the neighbors; all this talk of rebuilding must be snuffed out.

Therefore, the Israelites have been under constant attack from every side—Sanballat and the Samaritans from the North, Tobiah and the Ammonites from the East, Geshem and the Arabs from the South, and the Ashdodites from the West. Nehemiah 4:8 tells us they've formed a kind of dark alliance to bring pressure on the construction workers. And the greatest weapons in their arsenal are fear and discouragement.

But God has different ideas. He has empowered his visionary servant Nehemiah in a mighty way; day by day, the work goes on. Brick by brick the walls are rising again. Here in the fourth chapter of Nehemiah, as we join the story, the work is halfway complete. The people can smell victory. And yet the wisdom of experience tells us that the midpoint is a precarious place to be. A bit less than half, or a bit more than half, isn't so bad; but it's dangerous to be exactly in the middle. Johnny Mercer's old song "Accentuate the Positive" says, "Don't mess with Mister In-Between."[2] That's actually rather profound.

The Bible tells us that right in between, at the halfway point, a fresh wave of discouragement broke out through rumors of marauders and mayhem. Nehemiah realized that he must deal with the lagging spirits of his people. I think you'll recognize that the principles he used haven't changed. Nehemiah had to deal with discouragement in the same ways we do. As we review these principles, you're likely to say, "Oh yes—I've been there; I've done that."

Let's discover how Nehemiah handled the problem.

RECOGNIZING DISCOURAGEMENT

Recognizing what makes us vulnerable to discouragment is the first step to keeping it at a distance. Here are four factors that can lead us to losing heart.

FACTOR ONE: FATIGUE

Vince Lombardi observed that "fatigue makes cowards of us all." The wall-builders found that to be true. "The strength of the laborers is failing," said Judah (Nehemiah 4:10).

The construction project required fifty-two days of back-breaking labor. Halfway finished, the workers had been going at it for a month. Fatigue was catching up with them, and when energy runs short, so does courage.

Haven't you found this to be true? You're working twelve-hour days, finishing the annual report. You're working on weekends. Or you're cleaning the house all day, then helping the kids with algebra homework at night. For a while you'll rock along, doing what you feel you must. But sooner or later your personal limits will catch up with you. Every human body is governed by its own mathematical formula involving time, pressure, and exertion. If you exceed the limits of that equation, the cracks start to appear. You begin to be tense, irritable, and gloomy. Those are the times when your enemy, the devil, circles your name on his agenda.

As I've become older, I hope I've grown wiser. One little bit of wisdom I've grasped is that I can no longer push myself as hard as I used to. I'm an odd one to be lecturing to you on this topic, for I've always been a type A personality. I doubt that will change. But these days I see the importance of pacing myself. I need to build a little more margin in my life, and I need to protect those margins; otherwise, if I push too hard for too long, I'm going to see diminishing returns on the investment of my time and talents—and then comes the deluge of discouragement.

That certainly happened in Jerusalem. The people were weary, discouraged, and one other thing—they were frustrated.

FACTOR TWO: FRUSTRATION

We've just seen Judah's complaint in the first part of verse 10, when he observed that the workers' strength was failing. He continued, "There is so much rubbish that we are not able to build the wall."

Have you ever worked for days and weeks on mundane details, then stepped back and wondered if your efforts had any significance? Tired as they were, the Israelites no longer saw the proud, gleaming walls of their dreams. Visions of glory seemed like a mirage in the desert. There was nothing but broken bricks, mud, and debris. The tenth verse records that they were suddenly frustrated with the ever-present rubbish and rubble of heavy construction. Have you ever noticed how ugly a building site can be? There will be a sign with a beautiful painting of a glass tower, sparkling in the sunshine—and behind the sign is an ugly hole in the mud. At Jerusalem, the old walls had been torched. Now there were great piles of worthless debris everywhere.

The frustration of those endless mountains of rubble was weighing on Nehemiah's people. They would nearly collapse in weariness as the sun went down. Then, arriving for work the next morning, it would appear to them as if nothing had been accomplished. It seemed as if the debris had a life of its own and was multiplying. They were *burned out*.

That's a buzzword of our times: *burnout*. We all use it. In past generations, a man might work his entire adult life at one trade for one employer, then retire after fifty years with the gold watch; if he ever felt "burned out" along the way, there wasn't the word to articulate it. Today, we're always shifting careers and pointing to burnout. I've heard it said there are three ways to live: you can *live out*, you can *wear out*, or you can *burn out*. I'm hoping to live out, and I'm sure you'll agree that's the best alternative.

But we need to define this concept of burnout with care. I hear people use the word to mean *working too hard*. That's not a definition of burnout. Many of my friends work hard and energetically without ever burning out, because they work with focus and perspective. They have something called *vision*, and they move forward toward attainable goals.

The true nature of burnout is working too hard at the wrong thing. It's striving for a goal you can't accomplish— perhaps a goal no one can accomplish. Burnout is pulling the whole weight uphill all by yourself, reaching the summit, and realizing you're only going to topple to the bottom to start all over again. It's a feeling of despondency, and Nehemiah's workers were suffering from rubbish burnout. They couldn't see the picture of the shining city, only the debris. In a word, they were frustrated.

FACTOR THREE: FAILURE

Nehemiah 4:10 tells us so much. "The strength of the laborers is failing [fatigue], and there is so much rubbish [frustration] that we are not able to build the wall [failure]."

The Israelites threw up their hands here and pronounced their failure. Fatigue and frustration are a good recipe for failure. "We're tired," they said. "We're fed up. We can't do this. It was a great idea, but we've been at it for a month and we can't take any more." Negative talk was infectious, spreading like a virus to infect a community.

Importantly, Nehemiah's people hadn't failed at all, but it *appeared* that way to them. Failure is one of life's giants, so let's look at it as a force for discouragement.

Failure is universal. Every human being who has ever

lived—with one exception, two thousand years ago—has succumbed to failure. What makes the difference is how we handle our failure. The great danger is in letting our negative thoughts and impressions be compounded by the adversity we suffer. When things go wrong we're more willing to give an ear to the Enemy, the world's greatest de-motivational speaker, and we slowly but surely begin to buy into his lies and distortions.

"I haven't accomplished anything at all," we murmur. "I'm a failure."

FACTOR FOUR: FEAR

Read the words of Nehemiah 4:11–12: "And our adversaries said, 'They will neither know nor see anything, till we come into their midst and kill them and cause the work to cease.' So it was, when the Jews who dwelt near them came, that they told us ten times, 'From whatever place you turn, they will be upon us.'"

We explored this topic of fear in the first chapter, but fear has something to do with discouragement too. Imagine the weary workers in Jerusalem, building their walls in the midst of all the ugly rubble. The job was grueling enough, but there was also the matter of these neighbors stopping by to put a word in their ear. These visitors were saying, "We've got a few surprises in store for you. You won't know when, you won't know how, but just when you least expect it, we'll slip in and kill you. And we'll take you out by increments, one by one, until the walls stand half-built with no one left to complete them."

Nothing derails the work of God's people like a negative word. Everyone who tries to serve the Lord knows the truth of this. I receive my fair share of critical letters. Someone hears me on the radio, or someone sees something we've published, and they attack. It goes with the territory of having a large ministry. But it's interesting to me how the Enemy always knows just when to put one of those letters on my desk. They come in times of struggle. They come at the In-Between Moment, when we're just about to regain our focus and move forward for God's kingdom again.

That's when the venomous words always materialize from some quarter. We're tempted to say, "So that's how people feel. Well, maybe I ought to just turn in my Bible and quit."

Criticism is toxic. Perhaps you're coping with it right now. Perhaps the bitter words of others are eroding your spirit in the workplace or even your home. Perhaps there are people who play on your fears until you become very discouraged.

RESPONDING TO DISCOURAGEMENT

Now that we've recognized all the factors that lead to discouragement, how can we respond?

FIRST RESPONSE: CRY OUT TO GOD

> "Hear, O our God, for we are despised; turn their reproach on their own heads, and give them as plunder to a land of captivity! Do not cover their iniquity, and do not let their sin be blotted out from before You; for they have provoked You to anger before the builders . . . Nevertheless we made our prayer to our God."
>
> —Nehemiah 4:4–5, 9

In the midst of discouragement, Nehemiah cried out to God. That was his first solution for keeping the faith and leading others to press forward when it seemed like their world was being turned upside down.

I'm going to make a radical suggestion to you. Next time you encounter some major setback in your life, reverse your usual procedure—that is, cry out to God *first* instead of *last*. Most of us wait until we've exhausted all other alternatives before appealing to God as a last resort. I don't know about you, but I grit my teeth when I hear someone say, "We've tried everything; now all we can do is pray."

Don't wait until last to look up. When discouragement comes, start at the top! Go to the Lord and ask Him to help you sort through all the issues. May I tell you what works for me in times of discouragement? I sit down with my computer and my journal and I begin to talk to God. I say, "Lord, I need to talk with You right now. Some things are going on in my life that I can't understand, and I'm having a hard time with it. I need to tell You about it."

For me, it helps to begin setting the issues down in writing as I verbalize my feelings to God. As I do this, something begins to change in my spirit.

First of all, I bring everything out of that dark "anxiety closet" into the light. Writing it down and reading it out loud brings clarity. I discover that things weren't quite the way I thought when they were smoldering within me. I've imposed order on them, examined them in the light.

Second, I've done as Nehemiah did—I've cried out to God. This is the most important thing. Sometimes we just need to let go, be a child, and cry out to our heavenly Father. That brings the innocence and dependence that are the beginning of wisdom. Doing so cuts through our discouragement. If you don't think this is a very spiritual approach, read through the psalms. When David was beset by worries (and he was beset by a multitude of them), he did exactly what I've prescribed. He wrote them down and cried them out. He was brutally honest about his discouragement, and you can be too.

SECOND RESPONSE: CONTINUE THE WORK GOD HAS GIVEN YOU TO DO

> So we built the wall, and the entire wall was joined together up to half its height, for the people had a mind to work.
>
> —Nehemiah 4:6

Why is it that our immediate reaction to adversity is to quit? Like the angry little boy on the playground, we take our ball and go home. People leave churches; they quit jobs; they walk away from marriages—all because they've encountered the predictable season of discouragement. And of course, that's the worst thing we can do. We always come to regret our emotional walkouts. Satan knows that if he can play on our emotions and get us to quit, he can keep the problem from being resolved. He can keep God's work from moving forward.

But take a look at Nehemiah. He felt all the discouragement of his people, but he never set down the trowel, never missed a beat in laying the next brick. He knew he had to keep on keeping on. Yes, there were problems to deal with—but he wasn't going to set aside the mandate God had given him. "The people had a mind to work," the Scriptures tell us. Nehemiah helped them see that productive labor is sometimes just what the doctor ordered. It's healthy and therapeutic to work off our frustration, even when life seems upside down. Maybe *especially* when life seems upside down.

Needless to say, continuing to press forward is also a great way to bring a little discouragement to the Enemy. Later on in the rebuilding process, Sanballat and Geshem tried one more stunt to make Nehemiah slow down on his work. They invited him to a conference. Anyone in the business world will tell you that conferences and committees are great ways to slow down productivity! I've always loved Nehemiah's comeback. "So I sent messengers to them, saying, 'I am doing a great work, so that I cannot come down. Why should the work cease while I leave it and go down to you?'" (Nehemiah 6:3).

Modern translation: "Please accept my regrets, but God's agenda outweighs yours right now." The main thing is to keep the main thing as the main thing. We need to have a firm grasp on what God called us to do, put on the blinders, and keep plugging away. As we've seen, clear goals are the best preventive maintenance for burnout.

No matter how devastated you may feel, no matter how down in the dumps your spirit may be, keep up the good work. Keep the faith. Experience leads me to believe that the times we *least* feel like working are the times we most certainly *should*. Emotions are treacherous advisers. We need to be disciplined and stay on task. Nehemiah knew his people didn't need to bail; they needed to build. They didn't need to walk; they needed to work. When we follow their example, our discouragement will have a way of sorting itself out.

THIRD RESPONSE: CONCENTRATE ON THE BIG PICTURE

> Therefore I positioned men behind the lower parts of the
> wall, at the openings; and I set the people according to their
> families, with their swords, their spears, and their bows.
> And I looked, and arose and said to the nobles, to the lead-
> ers, and to the rest of the people, "Do not be afraid of them.
> Remember the Lord, great and awesome, and fight for your
> brethren, your sons, your daughters, your wives, and your
> houses."
>
> —Nehemiah 4:13–14

Nehemiah's men were fanned out across the perimeter,
working on little sections of the wall—and that was part of the
problem. They were so separated that they couldn't commu-
nicate and encourage one another. They could see only their
own little hole in the wall, their own little pile of rubbish. It
was very difficult to maintain any perspective.

We, too, tend to reduce the world to the cubicles we work
in. "A desk is a dangerous place from which to watch the
world," said John le Carré. Your cubicle may not have a win-
dow, but you can always keep one wide-open in your spirit.
Open it to God. Open it to others. Hold on to the Big Picture.
Nehemiah's workers were down and out. The muddy bricks
and old debris made a discouraging picture, but only a few
steps back and a little imagination upward revealed a portrait
of the New Jerusalem. You may see nothing but drudgery in
your life; you need to see what He is doing in you, with you,
and for you. You need to hold on to that hope. It will help you
prevail in the darkest of times.

Nehemiah 4 shows how Nehemiah handled the problem. He positioned the people along the wall in rows. Suddenly they could see the unity of their workforce, the proud line standing firm along the walls. Can you see a mental picture of that? Now the workers could see that every man meant one more section of the wall under repair. Add it all up, and the total was a new city.

I once saw a cartoon filled with a crowd of hundreds of little characters packed together, all looking perplexed, all with identical thought bubbles above their heads, countless thought bubbles, all reading, "What can one man do?" From our side of the cartoon panel we can see how ludicrous that is. Each little man is in his own private torment, and yet they're not only an "each"—they're an army, if only they could see it. Don't let the Enemy isolate you.

Erma Bombeck is sorely missed. For thirty years she wrote a popular syndicated newspaper column, published fifteen books, received numerous awards, appeared regularly on *Good Morning America*, and gave a great voice to millions of people. I miss that voice, for it brought laughter and hope to all of us. But few of her admirers were aware of the sufferings she experienced. She had breast cancer, a mastectomy, and kidney failure. She worked through her trials, one by one, and maintained her grasp of the Big Picture. She once wrote,

> I speak at college commencements, and I tell everyone I'm up there and they're down there—not because of my successes but my failures. Then I proceed to spin all of them off—a comedy record album that sold two copies in Beirut . . . a sitcom that lasted about as long as a dough-

nut in our house . . . a Broadway play that never saw Broadway . . . book signings where I attracted two people: one who wanted directions to the restroom and the other who wanted to buy the desk. What you have to tell yourself is this: "I'm not a failure. I failed at doing something." There's a big difference . . . Personally and career-wise, it's been a corduroy road. I've buried babies, lost parents, had cancer and worried over kids. The trick is to put it all in perspective . . . and that's what I do for a living.[3]

She did it very well; that's why we loved her so deeply. She made us laugh at ourselves and think about life in perspective. She made us look up for a moment from the little holes in the walls that define our piece of geography. She helped us remember we're all a part of something bigger.

Pastor and futurist Leith Anderson wrote the following in his book *Leadership That Works*:

In the heat of a tough leadership battle it is easy to lose hope, become pessimistic, and convince ourselves of defeat. . . . But as Christians we must open our eyes to see the view from where Jesus sits. . . . When I am discouraged and my hope runs thin, I remember that I am part of something much bigger than I am, and much more important than the local church of which I am a part. I belong to the church of Jesus Christ, and the gates of Hell will not overcome it (Matthew 16:18). Seeing the worldwide kingdom of God, not just my little corner of it, is enormously encouraging to me. It builds my faith and strengthens my hope.[4]

From there, Anderson details example after example of good things coming to pass in the world because of Christ and His church. He takes us on a quick journey across the globe, and we see the many countries where souls are coming to salvation at phenomenal rates.[5]

The world is filled with voices of discouragement, but there is one place where we can always go to be uplifted.

FOURTH RESPONSE: CLAIM THE ENCOURAGEMENT OF GOD'S PROMISES

"Do not be afraid of them. Remember the Lord, great and awesome, and fight for your brethren, your sons, your daughters, your wives, and your houses."

—Nehemiah 4:14

In times of discouragement, run—don't walk—to the Word of God. You may hear yourself say something like, "I'm too low for Bible reading today. My heart wouldn't be in it." That's the point! When your heart is ailing, it needs a transfusion of hope and power. I tell people to learn the principle of force-feeding: get the book out, open it up, sit yourself down, tune your mind in, and read the Word aloud. These are practical things you can do; don't wait for your feelings, for you can act your way into feeling more easily than you can "feel" your way into acting.

I know how hard that can be. I have those mornings when my spirits are at low ebb as I approach my appointment with God. I speak to Him very frankly: "Lord, I need something special from You today. I'm going through a rough place here.

I want more than words on a page; more than ideas and spiritual concepts. I need You. I need Your voice. And so I'm asking You to meet me in Your Word today, Lord."

There are also times when I've said, "I refuse to put this Book down until I hear from You, Lord." Don't you think He's pleased by your yearning to know Him? He's going to answer you if you approach with a determined heart. He's going to help you see just what you need to see in His Word, and He's going to give you the grace that will help you prevail through the bumps in the rocky road of life.

Remember, the Bible is no ordinary book. God's Spirit dwells in its pages, and He wants you to find Him in passages like this one:

> God is our refuge and strength,
> A very present help in trouble.
> Therefore we will not fear,
> Even though the earth be removed,
> And though the mountains be carried
> Into the midst of the sea;
> Though its waters roar and be troubled,
> Though the mountains shake with its swelling.
> —Psalm 46:1–3

We can run to the New Testament too. In 2 Thessalonians 3:13, we discover that it's possible to become discouraged even while doing all the right things: "But as for you, brethren, do not grow weary in doing good." Those words *grow weary* carry the meaning of discouragement. This is a remarkable idea and one I find very helpful. You may be out visiting the sick, engaging in prison ministry, teaching Sunday school, working with needy people, or any other good deed. You may be serving Christ with all your heart and still become discouraged. The Bible says don't grow weary in your service.

And why? Look to Galatians 6:9 for the answer. "And let us not grow weary while doing good," that verse repeats, then adds, "for in due season we shall reap if we do not lose heart"—that is, if we do not *become discouraged*. You see, we find ourselves feeling low because we've lost perspective about whom we're serving, why we're doing it, and how God plans to reward us. We need to remember the reaping.

Don't lose sight of those things. Run to God's Word, keep your nose in the Book, and draw the strength you need to keep the faith and keep running your race.

FIFTH RESPONSE: CARRY SOMEONE ELSE'S BURDEN

Let's come back to Nehemiah and his massive renovation project. If we read a bit further into the fourth chapter, we'll find something very moving. We'll find a pattern of people helping one another.

Nehemiah's band of stragglers, the remnant of fallen Israel, had bonded together to become a team. They were unified in commitment. Some were carrying, some were guarding, some were building, and all of them were wearing swords. The final word of this passage is that they stayed up all night; they were too caught up in their work to go home for the evening. Nehemiah told us they didn't even change clothes except for washing. United we stand. They understood that if they were to prevail, they'd need to watch one another's backs. They'd need to help the weaker ones carry and help the shorter ones reach. They'd need to fill in for those who were older and wearier. They carried one another's burdens.

Discouragement tends to cut us off from doing this. It sends us inward, where pity parties are common and perspective is rare. How often I've forgotten my own little worries when I've been busy calling on someone who was sick or making my rounds at the hospital. Going in, I've told God that I had nothing to give these people; coming out, I've felt abundantly blessed. Our own burdens become lighter when we've been carrying the burdens of others. That's the way God planned things. He doesn't want you to bear your own load. He wants you to join a burden-bearing community. He wants you to be entrenched in a network of encouragement.

Do you need encouragement right now? My best advice to you is to go encourage someone else. Are you caught up in your own needs? Go fill the needs of others. You'll reap what you sow, and the love you give will return to you.

But some people have actually told me, "I don't know anyone who needs encouragement." Would you like to know the very best place to find them? In your church.

Fred Smith, a businessman, asked a church usher about his responsibilities. The man said, "Nothing more than being there, shaking hands, finding my place in the aisle, taking the offering, and showing up for an occasional ushers meeting." Smith thought this didn't sound very biblical, but he observed in the conversation that this man had a passion about the ministry of hospitality. So many people come to church filled with cares and anxiety, the usher had noticed, and they need a warm handshake, a listening ear, perhaps a hug. The man had found his place to serve God quietly but profoundly.[6]

This weekend, make it a project to go to church simply as an encourager. Ask God to direct your steps to someone who needs a dose of love.

When the world seems upside down, look for burdens to bear. You'll find your heart lifted. Pull your eyes away from the discouragement you feel, and place them on the courage others have shown—others like Doretha, whose husband shot her son in a drunken accident. There were many dark months before she came to the end of her despair. One evening at midnight it all came crashing in on her. She fell to her knees in her bedroom and called out, "Lord, help me! I'm tired of living this miserable life." It seemed as if the weight of the world had been on her shoulders. But having called out to God, she felt a certain dizziness. There was something different inside her; she knew she could sleep, and that's what she did—deeply, restfully. She began the next day as a new creature. She felt so much lighter that she actually looked in the mirror to see if she'd lost weight. Her shape was the same as always; it was her face that was new. It *glowed*.

Doretha couldn't comprehend the newness of things. She wanted to understand the change that had come across her, but she was a bit embarrassed to ask. In a little secondhand bookshop she found a book entitled *Here's Hope: Jesus Cares for You—The New Testament*. That word *hope* seemed to leap out at her. That's what was different about today. She took the book home with her and began to read hungrily. It wasn't long before she came across these words: "Come to Me, all you who labor and are heavy laden, and I will give you rest" (Matthew 11:28).

"God changed my whole life," Doretha told me, "mended my broken heart, saved my husband in jail, brought me and my husband closer together, showed us how to love and be loved—and not to take life for granted. Jesus is the hope of the world. God still answers prayer."

God brought Doretha and her husband into blessed light from the deepest of holes, and I have no doubt He can do the same for you. The depth of the hole can never compare to the depth of His love, the reach of His arms, and the height of His glory.

Let's come into those arms, all of us who are heavy-laden, and feel the lightness of casting our burdens down, until our faces shine with the brightness of Doretha's.

CHAPTER 3

WIN AGAINST WORRY

Your local YMCA is crowded with people who have come to relax. They take refreshing swims or work up a healthy sweat in the weight room. It's a place where you go for recreation—unless you happen to be the man in charge. George McCauslin directed a YMCA facility in the Pittsburgh area, and things weren't going well for him. The job was eating him up inside.

George was struggling with his work. The club's membership was on a downward spiral. It was operating in the red with high debt, and George had to contend with critical staff problems. People came here to work off their tension, but where could the director go with his own?

He went nowhere at all, of course. George worked obsessively, feeling that if he simply put in a little more time, he

51

could somehow put together all the pieces. It wasn't long before he was behind his desk eighty-five hours per week. And somehow, when he finally came home, he was too tired to sleep; he was already thinking about an early start for the next day. Vacations were few, and when he was away, the YMCA and its problems weighed even more heavily on his slumping shoulders. A therapist told him that something had better give because a nervous breakdown was well on its way.

That's when George began to think about God. Where did He fit into this unhappy, chaotic picture?

Daniel was a promising college student. At age nineteen he had committed his life to serving Christ, and his sights were set on entering the ministry. All around him were fun-loving students—just kids, really—who were soaking up all the good things about the college life and its atmosphere. But not Daniel; he was struggling to simply keep a meal down. His stomach was tied in knots, and it had been months since he'd enjoyed dinner without the fear of terrible stomach pain. The doctor did some tests and told Daniel he had the beginnings of a serious ulcer.

An ulcer—at age nineteen? Weren't those for fast-lane executives and Wall Street traders?

No, said the doctor. Ulcers are for chronic worriers. And Daniel knew he was speaking the truth. It seemed as if the mildest thing could cause him to snap—a car that wouldn't start, a textbook he couldn't find. He was as tight as a bowstring. And he was dwelling in the world of the worst-case scenario. *What if this, what if that? What's the worst that can happen?*

Daniel knew his health had been compromised, but, just as damaging, so had his joy. Wasn't he supposed to be living the abundant life? Hadn't Jesus said His yoke was easy and His burden light? Surely this anxiety couldn't be a pleasing thing for God to look upon; surely the Lord must have better plans for His child.

WEIGHED DOWN

We can all agree that when it comes to membership in the human race, worry is part of the package. We also know that it's a useless and unhealthy vice. Corrie ten Boom used to recite a little couplet: "Worry is an old man with bended head, carrying a load of feathers which he thinks are lead." She understood that anxiety is ultimately foolish because it concerns that which isn't. It lives in a future that can't be foreseen. It deals in what-ifs and could-bes, speculation and possibility. And as long as we dwell on the worst-case scenario, we guarantee our own misery, for an extensive catalog of calamity is always within reach of the imagination.

The Bible chooses its language carefully when describing worry. The basic biblical word has the meaning of "to take thought" or "to be careful." Those are good things, at first glance. But the Greek gives us the word picture of a divided mind. The worrier has a mind torn between the real and the possible, the immediate and the potential. He's trying to fight the battle of life on two fronts, and he's bound to lose the war.

The worrier attempts to live in the future, and that presents him with two problems: the future isn't here, and the future isn't his. Nothing can be done, and no amount of worrying affects the issue one iota. The future is unknown, uncontrollable, and therefore irrelevant in terms of our peace of mind.

These truths are especially poignant when it seems as if our world is upside down. In such moments of distraction and despair, we are desperate to find something we can cling to that will offer some stability—some hope. Yet worry offers no such handholds because the future contains no such solidity.

When Jesus preached the greatest sermon of all history (found in Matthew 5–7), He was very clear on this issue of anxiety. In a nine-verse passage in Matthew 6, He uses the expression "Don't worry" three times. So if you'd like to have the teachings of Jesus on the subject of anxiety, we can state them in full in two words: *don't worry*. The next time you do give in to worry, you can ask yourself which section of that teaching you don't understand.

Before we take a close look at the passage in which Jesus discussed worrying, may I offer two simple disclaimers?

DON'T WORRY DOES NOT MEAN DON'T PLAN

It's true that in Matthew 6:34 Jesus says, "Do not worry about tomorrow." The King James Version has it as, "Take therefore no thought for the morrow," and many people have seized on that as a prohibition against career ambition, financial planning, life insurance, or any number of things. But no one who takes the time to read the Gospels would say that Jesus has a problem with planning. He planned for His ministry after His death, resurrection, and ascension. He spent plenty of time preparing His disciples for Jerusalem and beyond.

He also taught that we shouldn't break ground on that new high-rise until we've done the paperwork (Luke 14:28). To live without planning isn't pure spirituality; it's pure insanity.

DON'T WORRY DOES NOT MEAN DON'T BE CONCERNED

There are those who quote Philippians 4:6 ("Be anxious for nothing") as an excuse for a careless lifestyle. "Don't worry, be happy." But that's not what we're talking about at all. If you don't worry about your children playing near traffic, you're a terrible parent. If you're not concerned about walking off the roof of a skyscraper, you'll learn the meaning of that old poster that said, "Gravity: It's not just a good idea. It's the law." There are things you need to be concerned about. There's a difference between carefree and careless.

But realistic concern and restless anxiety are separate matters. So what is the difference? In short, concern focuses on the present; worry is attached to the future. The present is before us, and there are actions we can take. The future is out of our hands.

What Jesus is teaching about is the captivity of worry, and in Matthew 6 we'll discover what worry is all about and how we can face it as part of our efforts to keep the faith and finish our race.

FACING WORRY

We're going to explore one of the most encouraging and comforting of all Jesus' teachings. It's part of the Sermon on the Mount, and it's actually divided into two sections—verses 25–32, then verses 33–34. Let's find out what is revealed in the first of those sections.

WORRY IS INCONSISTENT

"Therefore I say to you, do not worry about your life, what you will eat or what you will drink; nor about your body, what you will put on. Is not life more than food and the body more than clothing?"

—Matthew 6:25

Worry is simply inconsistent. Jesus is asking, "Who gave you the body you live inside? Who established its requirements—for food, for clothing, for shelter? Do you think He has gone anywhere? Don't you think that same Provider will see to your needs?"

In essence, this is an argument from the greater to the lesser. Consider the God who created us a little lower than the angels, ordaining and establishing the miracle of human life in all the beautiful complexity of the human organism. Then He fashioned with His powerful hands the heat of the sun, the revolving world, and the four seasons. He took an awful lot of trouble, didn't He? Why, then, would He be careless about these little things—a crust of bread, a patch of clothing, a dry haven from the storm? A God so tall could never overlook something so small, according to Jesus. "Is not life more . . . ?" Those are His words.

If you buy into a Creator God, you must buy into a Sustainer God—or you're simply inconsistent. The evidence of His loving and timely care is all around us. Use your mind and you'll find comfort for your soul.

WORRY IS IRRATIONAL

"Look at the birds of the air, for they neither sow nor reap nor gather into barns; yet your heavenly Father feeds them. Are you not of more value than they?"

—Matthew 6:26

Jesus' first argument is irrefutable. He who gave us life can surely sustain that life. But Jesus has anticipated the follow-up question: God *can* provide, but *will* He provide?

Jesus attacks this second question from the opposite direction. Now He moves from the lesser to the greater—in this case, from birds to human beings. He says, "Look into the trees and you'll see the little sparrows. A plain copper coin will buy you two of them. Few things are sold so cheaply. Does your Father value you less than a copper coin? His hand is behind every bird that falls to the ground; if He's got the whole world in His hands, doesn't that include you?" (Matthew 10:29, paraphrase).

Sometimes we make fascinating discoveries when we bring two separate Scripture passages together. Consider this matter of the value of sparrows. Take a side trip over to Luke 12:6, and you'll find another market value: five sparrows for two copper coins. Put Matthew and Luke together and it's two for a penny and "buy four / get one free."

A copper coin was worth one-sixteenth of a denarius; a denarius was one day's wages. So what Jesus is saying is this:

"A copper coin gets you two sparrows; two coins get you five. Not even the free sparrow, who has no market value, can fall to the ground without your Father knowing about it. He follows every movement, whether it's bird or beggar or baron."

As a matter of fact, says Jesus, if He knows every sparrow that falls to the ground, He knows when one of your hairs does likewise. Somewhere He has a database that tracks the very hairs on your head. And if He is so meticulous with the smallest, most incidental inventory items, won't He also tend to your deeper concerns?

Once again, Jesus gives us an argument we can't refute, this time from the lesser to the greater. We must conclude that worry is inconsistent and irrational. But there's another problem with it.

WORRY IS INEFFECTIVE

"Which of you by worrying can add one cubit to his stature?"
—Matthew 6:27

Have you noticed all the units of measure in this passage? It's fascinating how Jesus deals with the concept of anxiety by calling on various lengths and weights and values. It's because when we deal with worry, we're dealing with matters of perspective and true worth. So we have coin and cubit, hair and sparrow.

A cubit, as Noah knew, comes to about eighteen inches— the length of your forearm, since rulers and yardsticks were rare in those days. There are two possible interpretations of Jesus' point here. One is, "Who can sit back in his chair and worry himself a few extra inches in height?" If that were possible, the implications for basketball would be profound. But it's not possible, and I say that with some regret. When I was growing up, I watched the great players of the NBA and wanted to add a cubit—well, at least a few inches—to my height. I was six foot one, and I wanted badly to be six five. But no amount of dreaming, no amount of yearning, could add an inch to my height. Wilt Chamberlain's and Bill Russell's jobs were safe.

That interpretation of the verse seems clear, but perhaps Jesus was going a bit deeper. What if we're talking about days instead of inches—futures instead of forearms? "Which of you by worrying," He might be saying, "can add a day to your life?" The answer, of course, is that we can't add a day, an hour, or a flickering moment. Worry divides the mind and multiplies misery. It subtracts from our happiness. But it never adds.

What if we took a walk through the cemetery in your community and discovered that each tombstone included a gauge indicating the years of life that person lost through worrying? We might be amazed. Could it be that some of us take five, ten, or fifteen years off our longevity by the force of gravity weighing us down with needless anxiety? I've known a few of these individuals. I've counseled people who have worried themselves out of this world early, simply because they couldn't leave things in God's hands.

Worry is the most ineffective use of your time. A friend of mine told me about visiting his brother, who kept a little white mouse in a cage. The mouse could climb onto the inside of a big wheel, and as he ran the wheel spun 'round and 'round. My friend's brother said, "It's fun to watch this little guy. It's as if he wakes up and says, 'Must get on the wheel! Must keep running!'" The average pet mouse, we're told, will run nine thousand miles on such a wheel in his lifetime, and he's *still inside the cage.*

That's the way it is with worry—a lifetime of frantic running with no destination. After a while you run out of the strength God gave you, and you're still in the cage. "Worrying doesn't rob tomorrow of its sorrow," someone said. "It robs today of its strength."

WORRY IS ILLOGICAL

"So why do you worry about clothing? Consider the lilies of the field, how they grow: they neither toil nor spin; and yet I say to you that even Solomon in all his glory was not arrayed like one of these. Now if God so clothes the grass of the field, which today is, and tomorrow is thrown into the oven, will He not much more clothe you, O you of little faith?"

—Matthew 6:28–30

We can agree that worry is an unattractive thing, shabby and gloomy and careworn. But what does lightheartedness look like? Jesus gives us a clue in these verses. Have you walked through a beautiful garden in the springtime? It's very difficult to be weighed down by the cares of the world when you're surrounded by the majesty of God's beautiful art. Solomon was a glorious king, Jesus tells us, with the wealth of several kingdoms at his disposal. But all of his sparkling finery pales in comparison to the simplest lily that God placed beside your feet.

And how many office hours have those lilies put in? How many dues have they paid? Have you ever seen a lily suffering through an anxiety attack? They neither toil nor spin. They simply sway in the breeze, reaching heavenward toward the source of their water and sunshine and sustenance. They do neither more nor less than they were designed to do, and what they were designed to do is to glorify God. Would that you and I could glorify God with the simple eloquence of that little flower.

Yet the greater point is that God values you so much more than a lily. The lily is merely something He created for your pleasure, for you're the one that bears His image. If He cares for each petal or stem that blooms and fades within a season, how much more does He care for you? How much more does He take to heart the things that cause your anxiety?

He took the answer to that question and displayed it on a cross two thousand years ago. He'd never suffer and die for the same children He planned to neglect. That's why worry is illogical, and that's why we can press forward toward the finish line with confidence.

WORRY IS IRRELIGIOUS

"Therefore do not worry, saying, 'What shall we eat?' or 'What shall we drink?' or 'What shall we wear?' For after all these things the Gentiles seek. For your heavenly Father knows that you need all these things."

—Matthew 6:31–32

Inconsistent, ineffective, illogical, and *irrational* are concepts we can quickly latch onto. The next one requires a bit more contemplation for modern thinking, but it comes from the Word of God, and we must mold our minds to it. Jesus shows us that worry is irreligious.

What does *irreligious* mean? Isn't it true that the word *religion* is out of fashion among evangelicals today? Jesus' point is that to worry is to be just like everyone else—and "everyone else," to the Jew of that time, meant the Gentiles. There were two kinds of people: the Jews and everyone else. Through a special relationship with His special people, God had spent thousands of years demonstrating—through covenant and conquest, through wilderness and wandering, through kingdom and calamity—that He would be their God and they would be His people. Gentiles had no reason to believe such a thing, and it was natural for them to spend their lives in anxiety over food and shelter and clothing. But God's people should know better; it was written in bold letters across their law, proclaimed in their tabernacles, and should have been emblazoned in their hearts.

The goodness of God was the essence of their religion, and worry was a total denial of it. Worry denies our Father in heaven and our family on earth. It reduces us to the ways of the pagans who worship blind, deaf, and powerless idols; who live as if the desperation of a sacrifice at the altar will bring another few drops of rain. In the old days that might have been expressed in Baal worship, but it's just as alive today. We've simply removed the stone gods and replaced them with shiny new ones such as career, materialism, pleasure, and power—all the attainments we worry about in our denial that God will care for every need.

Do I ever worry? Of course I do; I've raised four children to adulthood, and that qualifies me as an expert on the subject.

But for me, worry is a small town I pass through, not a place to hang my hat. It's a momentary phase, not a lifestyle. For many people, worry becomes so ingrained in their personalities that, once the old worries are gone, they search for new ones. They've become dependent on worry as a lens through which to view life, and they've forgotten any other way to live. Do you want to become that kind of person? I know I don't.

Jesus is talking about our unbelief, and yet notice the tenderness of His words: "For your heavenly Father knows that you need all these things." He is saying, "Rest, take comfort. Every need you have is on God's agenda. Have you forgotten He is taking care of everything? Let your runaway mind come home and find rest."

FIGHTING WORRY

We find so many inconsistent, irrational, illogical, ineffective, and irreligious factors when we take a close look at worry. We have as much reason to avoid it as we do some deadly narcotic—for that's exactly what it is. But perhaps you've already become dependent upon that drug. Perhaps you need to become free from its tyranny.

How can you do it? Let me offer two suggestions.

YOU NEED A SYSTEM OF PRIORITIES

"But seek first the kingdom of God and His righteousness,
and all these things shall be added to you."

—Matthew 6:33

We've seen that the biblical prognosis of worry is a division of the heart. It's a mistake to try dealing with the issues of today while dwelling on the questions of tomorrow. We need all our energy and concentration for the here and now.

And where do we find Jesus' words on worry? They're right in the center of His teaching on personal possessions. I don't think that's a coincidence. The great overriding issue, after all, is priorities. What is most important to your heart? Those who base their lives on the acquisition of things tend to be the ones saddled with anxiety. But Jesus has a simple prescription: get your priorities in order. Seek the things of God first; live the righteous life He would have you live. Focus right there, putting aside every distraction. Then, let the chips fall where they may. As you do so, everything you need will materialize ("all these things shall be added to you").

Can it truly be that simple? Could such a formula really work?

If not, then you might as well put your Bible away, for nothing else in it will stand up. This teaching goes to the very heart of the central message of Scripture. But if these words are true—as you and I confirm in our hearts—then life can be embraced with joy and exuberance. It's something to enjoy, not to worry about, and the what-ifs no longer have any power over us.

Keep the faith by seeking God's kingdom and His righteousness as your first priority, and all these other things (possessions and accomplishments and goals) shall be added to you.

Most of us know this verse; actually living it is another matter. When I worry, I know I'm guilty of violating the ringing declaration of Matthew 6:33. I know I'm failing to live out my beliefs. Maybe it's that way in your life. Maybe the cycle of worry has become so powerful that you can't seem to break it. If so, then you need to step back from the complex tangle of your life and ask yourself how you've ordered it. What are your priorities? Do you really trust the Father who loves you, or is it all simply lip service? Can you live out your belief that God is sovereign?

Rebuild your system of priorities, with God at the center of the structure. If you build from that brand of brick, you'll be sheltered from the storms of worry and stress.

YOU NEED A STRATEGIC PROGRAM

> "Therefore do not worry about tomorrow, for tomorrow will worry about its own things. Sufficient for the day is its own trouble."
>
> —Matthew 6:34

What we have here may be the most important ammunition of all—a systematic strategy to weed out your worry. Jesus is saying something quite interesting: you won't sink under the burden of today's crises, but tomorrow's agenda puts you over the weight limit. Have you ever tried to carry too many bags of groceries at the same time? After cleaning the eggs from your driveway, you'll know better—and next time you'll make two trips instead of one. Jesus tells us to carry today's bag today and make a fresh trip tomorrow.

Living in the present tense is an art. Do you know someone who's "not all there," for his or her eyes are focused on some invisible horizon? This person is preoccupied with absent problems. But have you ever known someone who lives completely in the present? Such people seem lively, full of energy and charisma and getting their money's worth out of every new thing that comes along, and you won't catch them worrying. That's how Jesus wants us to live—a day at a time. There's a reason God placed us within the moment, bracketed away from both the past and the future. They're both off-limits to us, and we need to post No Trespassing signs. The past is closed for good, and the future is still under construction. But today has everything you need. Come here and make your home.

Many years ago, a prominent physician by the name of William Osler made some wise observations about worry. Throughout his career he had observed the physical effects of worry upon the lives of his patients. He used an analogy about the careful design of an ocean liner. If the hull of the ship is pierced by means of some collision, the steel doors of the hold can be lowered so that only a portion of the ship is flooded. Then Dr. Osler wrote that we should design our lives just as carefully. We all have our unforeseen collisions, and we must learn how to lower the forward hold doors against dangerous tomorrows; we must lower rear hold doors against the past; and we must learn to live safe and dry in the compartment of today.[1]

> All the water in the world
> However hard it tried,
> Could never sink a ship
> Unless it got inside.

All the hardships of this world
Might wear you pretty thin,
But they won't hurt you one least bit
Unless you let them in.

—Anonymous

FOCUS ON THE PRESENT,
NOT THE PAST OR THE FUTURE

Here are four specific elements of Jesus' program against worry that will keep us running the race in the present only.

DON'T DWELL ON TOMORROW'S STRESS

Jesus told us that tomorrow will take care of itself. Take note also of this powerful word: "As your days, so shall your strength be" (Deuteronomy 33:25).

As your days go, so goes your strength. What does that mean?

I've walked with the people of my church through bankruptcy, disease, divorce, legal problems, and every variety of trial. People tell me, "I don't know how I can face it." And I'm never insensitive to their anguish; in no way do I minimize their crises. But I do share with them the rich practical wisdom of the Bible: *leave tomorrow alone*. When that day dawns, God will give you the grace and the strength you need for it. At the present time, you have the grace and the strength He has given you for today. Your calendar gives each day its own number. Live them in that order, just as God arranged them. Stay in one square at a time.

A friend of mine takes his family on long automobile trips across the country. He has two small children, and each day they look forward to the day's "treat." The treat consists of a little bag for each child with an inexpensive surprise—and a Scripture passage. As they undergo each daylong ride, they have a little surprise to look forward to in the form of a simple gift and an eternal truth from God's Word that the family will discuss together as they drive. Life's road trip holds the same for you and me. Each new day will bring a new little package from God, with a little grace-gift to refresh us and the always-present truth of God's Word. But you have to wait for each day to have that package in your hands.

We don't totally ignore the future. We plan and prepare. But calm preparation and obsessed anxiety are two different things. Lower the door in the forward compartment. Shut off the waters of tomorrow that always drain today of its strength.

Mark Twain once said, "I'm an old man and I've known a great many troubles, but most of them never happened." Future-based anxiety is empty.

DON'T DWELL ON YESTERDAY'S MESS

One thing is always true about yesterday—it's gone. It's complete. It's out of reach, and there's nothing we can do about it. My son was a quarterback in college football, and I can watch videotapes of his wins and losses. Instant replay is a cruel thing when our team doesn't come out on top. No matter how many times I run the tape, our team misses the tackle or drops the pass or stumbles just short of the goal line. Every time I play it back, something in me thinks that this time the play may come out differently. But once the whistle has blown, the play is over, and we have to let it go.

That's difficult to do sometimes, isn't it? I know believers who have come to Christ from very troubled, perhaps sordid backgrounds. Occasionally the past creeps up on them and the Enemy whispers, "Don't forget who you were and what you did—you haven't really changed." Guilt is powerful. I remind these people of the infinite forgiveness of God. He has placed our past sins as far from us as the east is from the west. God has forgiven us.

But still, people insist that they can't forgive themselves. At that point I observe, "That's amazing—you have a standard higher than God's!"

If He can cut away the past, we must be able to do likewise. If you've confessed it, it's been forgiven. Put it away forever and move on; imagine it's been buried in the bottomless ocean of God's grace, and it has no more power over you. You might as well worry about something that happened several hundred thousand years ago, for it has that much relevance.

DON'T DWELL ON YESTERDAY'S SUCCESS

It's possible to feel anxiety about positive things too. What if there were a time when everything seemed right in your life? What if you received that great award or had a wonderful experience in your youth or had a happier period in your family? An aging athlete can think back to the time when he had that little bit of extra speed or endurance that made him an all-star. We dwell on these things, lamenting the good old days and how they've passed away.

Paul the apostle, one of the most successful men who

ever lived, made an interesting declaration at the close of his life and career. He said that he hadn't achieved his great goal yet, but that he kept his focus on one thing: forgetting what was behind him and pushing forward to the one wonderful thing still before him, which was the high calling of Christ (Philippians 3). Paul could have sat in that prison and lingered in the scrapbook of his memories—the miracles, the young churches, the glorious spread of the gospel at his hands. But he put even those wonderful memories behind him because the future sparkled even brighter.

That's what you and I must do when the world seems upside down. We must dwell on the miracle of what lies before us today, this moment, this second. All else is dim by comparison.

DON'T DWELL ON YESTERDAY'S DISTRESS

This could be the hardest thing to do—letting go of our heartbreak.

Everyone is served their cup of sorrow in season. There's no avoiding that in this world. And a considerable portion of my work of ministry is holding the hands of people and walking with them through the valley of the shadow. But I hope I can help them walk finally back into the light, for that valley is no place to build a home. Grief and mourning are clean, biblical emotions, but they're not permanent ones. Every extra day of dwelling in those shadows is a day of joy lost—a day of not seeing the wonderful things God wants us to see.

The important thing is to keep on walking. Don't look over your shoulder to yesterday's happiness or sadness; don't crane your neck to see what may lie ahead. You need to put one foot in front of the other and take one step at a time. Live in the present tense, and make every day a beautiful gift to God, unmarred by the lines and wrinkles of worry.

An anonymous poet wrote,

> My name is I AM.
> If you live in the past,
> It will be very hard,
> For I am not there.
> My name is not I WAS.
> And if you live in the future,
> It will be very hard,
> For my name is not I WILL BE.
> But if you live in the present,
> It is not hard,
> For my name is I AM.

I saw a sign not too long ago that said Free Gas Tomorrow. What a deal! But when I returned the next day, the sign still said the same thing—and tomorrow was still a day away. It's always just beyond our reach. We might as well be fueled by the grace and strength God has made available to us just for this day.

J. Arthur Rank had a system for doing that. He was one of the early pioneers of the film industry in Great Britain, and he also happened to be a devout Christian. Rank found he couldn't push his worries out of his mind completely; they were always slipping back in. So he finally made a pact with God to limit his worrying to Wednesday. He even made himself a little Wednesday Worry Box and he placed it on his desk.

Whenever a worry cropped up, Rank wrote it out and dropped it into the Wednesday Worry Box. Would you like to know his amazing discovery? When Wednesday rolled around, he would open that box to find that only a third of the items he had written down were still worth worrying about. The rest had managed to resolve themselves.[2] I challenge you to make a worry box. Take some kind of action against worry.

George McCauslin knew he had to do something. The YMCA director's anxiety problem was a threat to his emotional health. He scheduled an afternoon off from work. With the hours he was putting in, that took a great deal of determination. George drove to the western Pennsylvania woods, a place he associated with peace and tranquility. He took a long walk, trying to empty his mind and concentrate on the fresh air and the pleasant aromas of nature. It was a good idea. His tight neck was relaxing, and he could feel the slightest few ounces of tension draining away. As he sat beneath a tree and pulled out his notebook, he breathed a long sigh. This was the first time in months he'd felt anything close to relaxation.

George felt as if he and God had grown far apart, so he decided to write his Creator a letter. "Dear God," he began. "Today I hereby resign as general manager of the universe." He read it back to himself and signed it, "Love, George."

George laughs as he tells the story. "And you know what happened? God accepted my resignation."[3]

Daniel, the college student beset by an anxiety-riddled stomach, did much the same thing. He packed up his little car and headed into the mountains for a two-day retreat with nothing but a sleeping bag, a canteen, and a Bible. He asked God to break through his torment during the retreat, and that's what happened. As he read the Gospels, he came to the verse we've already discussed: Matthew 6:33. For the first time, he really understood the vital significance of seeking first the kingdom. From that moment, he's had a battle plan for challenging his anxiety.

"As we become people who can praise the Lord in spite of our needs," he writes, "He has promised that we will become a people who will find their needs met."[4]

FOUR VERSES, SIX WORDS

I'd like to leave you with some weapons you can use against worry—four verses to help you when your mind is prone to anxiety, and six words to rally around. Copy the following verses down and keep them handy. Better yet, commit them to memory.

- "Call upon Me in the day of trouble; I will deliver you, and you shall glorify Me" (Psalm 50:15).
- "Cast your burden on the LORD, and He shall sustain you; He shall never permit the righteous to be moved" (Psalm 55:22).
- "Casting all your care upon Him, for He cares for you" (1 Peter 5:7).

And here is the pinnacle passage concerning worry:

Be anxious for nothing, but in everything by prayer and supplication, with thanksgiving, let your requests be made known to God; and the peace of God, which surpasses all understanding, will guard your hearts and minds through Christ Jesus.

—Philippians 4:6–7

And what are the six words of wisdom for worriers?

Worry about nothing—pray about everything!

Make those words your battle cry as you take on the giant of worry.

CHAPTER 4

DISARM YOUR DOUBTS

Four centimeters. How could four tiny centimeters make so much difference—cause so much suffering?

How could four marks on a metric tape so profoundly punish a family, strain a marriage, and call into question the very goodness of God?

"Your daughter has a condition called microcephaly," said the doctor. "Her head should have a circumference of thirty-five centimeters—but it measures only thirty-one."

For several days, Susan sat in the hospital pondering the ominous words. For now, nothing was sure. Mandy might lead a happy, normal life after all. But the uncertainty was cruel, almost intolerable. Marshall, her husband, was out of town. How could he be away at a time like this—a time when doctors were using words like *disability* and *severe*?

For weeks the Shelleys prayed intensely, desperately, unceasingly. Countless friends joined them in prayer. Marshall was the editor of a successful Christian magazine, and he was known and loved by many. But God didn't seem to be offering special favors to Christian editors; the weeks only confirmed everyone's deepest fears. The Shelleys' third child, it seemed, would never walk or talk, sit up, or even recognize her caregivers. Her life would be defined by seizures, rounds of hospitalization, and an infinite array of medications.

At the age of three months, cataracts were detected in Mandy's eyes. There was corrective surgery, but did it really matter? Susan couldn't be certain her daughter ever saw her face—or heard her voice, for that matter. Family life was totally dominated by care for the suffering and unresponsive child; it was an open-ended emergency, a crisis never resolved. Eight hours were often required simply to feed Mandy. Late-night hospital trips were routine.

Meanwhile, the tension only grew thicker between husband and wife. Where was God? *He's more than welcome to show up—any time now would be fine*, thought Marshall and Susan.

It was just then, in the midst of caring for Mandy, that the surprise came. Susan was pregnant again. Here, finally, was a ray of sunshine—a message that God approved of their strong faith in hard times. And the child would be their first boy.

In the fifth month, Susan went to see the doctor for an ultrasound. He brought this report: "The fetus has a malformed heart. The aorta is attached incorrectly. There are missing portions of the cerebellum. Clubfoot, cleft palate, and perhaps a cleft lip. Possibly spina bifida . . . This is a condition incompatible with life." The little boy was likely to spontaneously miscarry, but in any case he wouldn't survive long outside the womb. The doctor suggested a "termination," but Susan, still honoring God as the giver and taker of life, carried the child to term. The only time she would have for getting to know her little boy, she reflected, might well be a few short weeks in the womb.

The Shelleys turned their prayers to survival and healing for the child. Again, the community of faith encircled them with intercession and support. The little boy was born, took a deep breath, and turned blue. Two minutes after he entered the world, he quietly departed it again. His name was Toby, from the biblical *Tobiah*, which means "God is good." That wasn't how the family felt, but it was still what they believed.

In a few months, Mandy followed her tiny brother into the next world, and she was buried beside him; two tiny coffins, two graves, two aching losses.

Susan grieved bitterly for her double loss; her prayers were angry and accusing. If God couldn't take any better care of His children here on earth, how could she know they were better off now? People offered all the usual pat answers about God's allowance of suffering; none of these lines were good enough. Susan needed something for her *soul*. For three nights she lay awake, pleading for a simple thing: some assurance that Mandy and Toby were safe, whole, and cared for.

Just a simple answer would be enough; just a gesture from the Hand that was supposed to offer love; then perhaps she could let go. Susan prayed. And even more, she listened— listened through the silence.

THE QUESTION OF "WHY?"

Perhaps it's the defining question for our species: *Why?* Of all God's creatures, we are the only ones who seek to understand, to secure the reason and the rationale. Humanity will go to great lengths simply to find meaning. We challenge the atom; we push into space. But that meaning can be elusive. More essential questions haunt us: *Where is the child I've lost? Why am I here? What is the significance of my life? What would have happened if I'd chosen the other road—of marriage, of career, of faith?*

When the answers elude our grasp and the void ignores our questions, we suffer a kind of spiritual vertigo we call *doubt.* Suddenly all the assumptions on which we've built a life, large and small, are like a toothpick replica of the Eiffel Tower—pull out one support and, if it's close enough to the foundation, the whole structure topples. The world turns upside down. Every belief we have is threatened.

For most of us, it's in the aftermath of pain and shock that the questions come. *Why, Lord? Why?*

That word cruelly haunted the mother of Glenn Chambers. On February 15, 1947, that young man was waiting to board a DC-4 bound for Quito, Ecuador. Glenn was off to make his dreams come true; he was enlisting as a missionary through an organization called the Voice of the Andes. He had a few extra minutes before takeoff, so he looked for a scrap of paper on which to write a note to his mother. Then his plane disappeared into the clouds, never to emerge. It crashed into the peak of El Tablazo, near Bogotá. Consumed by flames, it hurtled from the skies into a ravine fourteen thousand feet below. The unthinkable news came to his mother—followed, a few days later, by his final note. He had scribbled it on the corner of an advertisement that happened to be dominated by one towering word: *Why?*

The word mocked and haunted the mother of Glenn Chambers. Here were his last known words, seemingly from beyond the grave. They were filled with cheer, ignoring those looming letters, black and blaring, that asked the unanswerable. The same letters stand poised in the backdrop of our own lives. We can't ignore them forever. Inevitably we must doubt.

The Greek words for *doubt* carry the idea of uncertainty. They have the connotation of being unsettled, of lacking a firm conviction. Doubt is not the opposite of faith but the opportunity of faith—the growing pains of an eager, seeking spirit. The true enemy of faith is unbelief, but doubt is a necessary leg of the journey. It stands at the edge of past understandings and stretches painfully for new frontiers.

To doubt, then, is to be human. We read the Bible and find doubters at every turn, even among the greatest of men— David, Job, Solomon, Jeremiah. In the New Testament we quickly come to the man known as John the Baptist, who demanded faith from his followers. He proclaimed answers in ringing oratories, but he also asked his share of questions. As he sat behind bars, under the arrest of King Herod, he found himself pondering deeply and darkly. He sent his men to Jesus with a question: "Are you the coming One, or do we look for another?"

John had been in the wilderness preaching his heart out, proclaiming the coming of the Deliverer. Jesus described him as the greatest "among those born of women"—quite an endorsement (Matthew 11:11). It had been a short time since John had baptized Jesus. It was a moment of supernatural power, and John heard the voice of God affirming Jesus as the Christ. But now, away from the crowds and the river baptisms, within the darkness of a prison cell, nothing seemed the same. The tables were turned, and John couldn't help but ask the question straight out: *Are You the real thing, or will all our hopes and dreams be shattered once again?*

If it could happen to the greatest man born of women, then none of us are exempt. Doubts are inevitable for the weak and the wise.

I was raised in a wonderful home by believing parents, but I grappled with my share of doubts through my adolescent years. As a matter of fact, doubts are basically guaranteed in Christian homes. The essentials of the faith are so ingrained, so taken for granted, that we must test them before making them our own.

No, the questioning spirit is not sinful, but simply a rite of passage we must all pass through as we grow into a deeper faith. God understands. He's far more pleased when we ask the questions and challenge the assumptions than when we accept, secondhand and prefabricated, the faith of our parents. That's not a living, breathing faith at all, but an heirloom to display in some corner of the living room with the other antiques. Your Father wants you to work out your salvation with fear, trembling, confrontation, tears, and whatever else might be required to nurture an authentic personal friendship with the living God.

Most of us need to reinstate that word *doubt* as a friend, not an enemy. But there's another word we need to examine: unbelief.

We might say that doubt asks questions; unbelief refuses to hear answers. The former is hard miles on a good journey; the latter is the dead end, a refusal to travel any farther.

DEALING WITH DOUBTS

John 20 brings us into the presence of history's most notorious doubter. His name was Thomas. The Bible often refers to him as Thomas *Didymus*. Many people assume the meaning is "Thomas the Doubter," but actually it means "Thomas the Twin." *Didymus* travels down through the years and comes to us in the English language as *ditto*—double. We have no idea what happened to Thomas's twin, but we know he was often "in two minds," which is one definition of doubt.

He was the classic skeptic, adamantly unwilling to accept anything on simple hearsay—not without a razor-sharp question or two. Perhaps in our time he would be a lawyer. But there was a touch of melancholy about Thomas as well, a bit of the pessimist. You and I may not have placed him on the short list for Jesus' executive cabinet, but the Lord selected Thomas as one of His closest friends. Perhaps He needed a tough-minded disciple, as all our organizations do.

I wish we had time to review all the references to Thomas in the Gospels. One will have to suffice. It was that unforgettable evening when Jesus and His followers met in the upper room for their final meal, recorded in John 14:4–5. Jesus was gently preparing His disciples for the suffering and tragedy to come, and He said, in essence, "You know where I must go, and you know how it must happen."

Thomas was the first with a reply, which we might para-phrase as, "Lord, we have no idea where You're going. How would we know something like that?" Skeptics don't buy into subtlety and elliptical references. They're lovers of straight talk, clear words, and hard answers.

That's the Thomas of Scripture—practical, skeptical, tak-ing nothing for granted, but *not* unbelieving. Thomas went everywhere the Twelve went. He saw and felt and heard all the miraculous events. He knew who could walk on water, who could raise a dead friend, who controlled the very winds of the storm. Surely the life of Thomas had been transformed along with the rest. But still he doubted. We can have faith, see miracles, and still have questions. As a matter of fact, the thinking believer will only have his questions increased when the miracles flow.

The defining moment in Thomas's life is found in John 20. For Peter, that moment came at a fish fry, when Jesus forgave him and sent him out to change the world. But for Thomas it happened here, in the room where the disciples had huddled together—the room that was entered in fear and departed in faith. This is the room where doubt was overcome and skepti-cism was left in awe.

Let's enter that room now and learn the timeless secrets of doubt and belief so that we can keep the faith even in our most discouraging of seasons.

DOUBT DEVELOPS IN ISOLATION

John 20:24 gives us the key to the passage: Thomas had missed the fireworks. Jesus had appeared in the midst of His friends, shown His wounds, and pointed toward the future.

Great joy and celebration had broken out in that room. Jesus alive? Could it be true? Yes, for He was right there in the flesh—but Thomas was not, and this is a significant point.

Ten men gathered together in the custom of the bereaved. When someone near to us dies, we rendezvous at someone's home; we bring food and gentle laughter and words of consolation. Solitude isn't recommended, for we need the encouragement available in the intermingling of our spirits. But Thomas, independent thinker that he was, had drawn apart and missed not only the consolation but also the miracle.

Doubt flourishes in the dark. It's a bit like those mushrooms that grow in damp cellars. It thrives on the cold, dank loneliness of the human spirit. In solitude, the questions seem larger, more ominous, more hopeless. Where was John the Baptist when he began to question the very content of all of his own preaching? He was in a dark cell, away from the throng, there in the dungeon where the mushrooms grew. Darkness feeds doubt; daylight has a way of dispelling the worst of it.

That's why doubt is a wise occasion for examining our feelings. Sometimes our questions have less to do with theological enigmas than with a simple case of the blues. Our souls and our bodies live in such close company that they tend to catch each other's diseases. Physical illness dampens the soul, and emotional depression causes bodily fatigue. C. S. Lewis admitted to struggling with doubt when he was on the road in some inn or strange bed. He loved his home and his circle of friends, and absence often brought on a fit of soul vertigo for him.

Stay connected to people and you're more likely to stay connected to your faith.

DOUBT DEMANDS EVIDENCE

True doubt never turns away from the facts, wherever they may lead. It stubbornly pursues the truth. It's Galileo questioning that the world is flat; Chuck Yeager insisting the sound barrier is no barrier at all; Thomas requiring a handling of the evidence.

> So he said to them, "Unless I see in His hands the print of the nails, and put my finger into the print of the nails, and put my hand into His side, I will not believe."
>
> —John 20:25

Consider the doubter's perspective. When Jesus had drawn up the group itinerary, Thomas had spoken against going to Jerusalem. As he saw things, it was simply too dangerous a place to visit—Jesus would die, and perhaps the disciples would die with Him. Sure enough, his direst predictions for Jesus had come true. If only they had listened to Thomas, master of the worst-case scenario. Skeptics draw a melancholy satisfaction from the words "I told you so."

Now, when the disciples were elbowing one another out of the way, shouting over one another to tell Thomas the incredible news (for we all love trumping the pessimist), how did Thomas respond? Just exactly as we'd expect—he recited the Skeptic's Creed. "I'll believe it when I see it," he said. "As a matter of fact, scratch that—I'll believe it when I *feel* it. You'll forgive me for not taking your word for it. I'll make my own evaluation, if it's all the same to you."

Just as we love chastising Peter for failing to walk on water—regardless of whether we would have stepped out of the boat—we're all too ready to condemn Thomas simply because he insisted on validation. At least he was honest; he called it as he saw it. He never called the disciples' claims impossible; he never ruled out miracles. He simply wanted to test the evidence personally.

As we'll see, Jesus met Thomas at the point of his questions. Ask God with an honest heart, and He'll always answer you.

DOUBT DRAWS US BACK TO CHRIST

Scene: the same room, but eight days later. For more than a week, the issue had separated Thomas and his friends. Had they witnessed the greatest event in history, or had they been cruelly deceived?

It's significant that Thomas, despite his reservation, had lingered among them. Here again is the difference between doubt and unbelief. Doubt says, "I'll stay and investigate." Unbelief stalks away and says, "Sure, you guys go on believing whatever you want. I'm out of here." Thomas stayed to ask the questions—and therefore received the answers.

> And after eight days His disciples were again inside, and Thomas with them. Jesus came, the doors being shut, and stood in the midst, and said, "Peace to you!"
>
> —John 20:26

Christianity ultimately comes down to something more than theological questions. In the end it's all about a Person, not a proposition. The questions are the beginning of the journey, but the answer comes finally in experience, in reaching out to touch and to feel and in being ourselves touched by the power of the nail-scarred hands. This is the experience of Thomas, who asked the right questions and whose doubts kept him among the community of faith and guided him across the room to the presence of the Savior.

The questions remain, of course. I'm sure if we could talk to the disciples, they wouldn't be able to fully explain the mysteries of Jesus' resurrection body that day—one that could move through walls even while displaying the scars of physical execution. After a while, such questions are moot. In the radiance of a Man fresh from conquering death, we're struck speechless, and we forget to ask about the little things. Too often we become ensnared in some element of doctrinal minutiae, forgetting the miracles that transcend the details.

I suspect that if Peter or John wandered by and caught a snatch of our arguments, they might say, "What's the point? Jesus descended to hell, broke the chains, and destroyed the power of death. Why the trivial pursuit in the living presence of Jesus?"

DOUBT DEEPENS OUR FAITH

Consider this: In the years to come, which disciple had the most definitive testimony of all? Who else plunged his hand into the jagged rift where the spear had been thrust? Who else ran a trembling finger along the slope of the wrists, where the nails had sliced through and splintered the wood? Who else would carry within his fingertips, for the rest of his life, the tactile memory of a resurrected body?

Only the doubter. Only Thomas.

Then He said to Thomas, "Reach your finger here, and look at My hands; and reach your hand here, and put it into My side. Do not be unbelieving, but believing."

—John 20:27

"But Peter," someone may have said, "your eyes played tricks on you."

"Don't you understand, John?" another might have offered. "We see what we long to see."

But Thomas knew, for his eyes and his hands offered consistent accounts. The Man before him was the friend he'd loved as a brother, the companion whose death was a matter of hard fact.

Assurance is the reward of the insistent seeker, and Jesus affirmed it on a separate postresurrection appearance.

And He said to them, "Why are you troubled? And why do doubts arise in your hearts? Behold My hands and My feet, that it is I Myself. Handle Me and see, for a spirit does not have flesh and bones as you see I have." When He had said this, He showed them His hands and His feet.

—Luke 24:38–40

Read those words well, for Jesus looks beyond the page and into your eyes, and He makes you the same offer. "Are you unsure? Reach in and feel for yourself." And with that, He shows you His hands and His feet—if you'll only reach out and touch.

Jacob was brash enough to wrestle an angel, and the angel

wrestled back; God is big enough to handle the questions that trouble you. Just be *honest* about your doubts. The Bible doesn't affirm those doubts you keep in the box on the shelf, unused, unexamined, that you bring out whenever someone invites you to church. Doubts, useless in and of themselves, are useful when they lead us somewhere.

I commend whoever said that we should believe our beliefs and doubt our doubts. That may sound trite to you, but I find a certain amount of wisdom in that phrase. Repressed doubt, stuck away in the closet, can become a devil's wedge. It's like the letter from the IRS that you're afraid to open. After a while, the emotional weight exceeds whatever peril the envelope could possibly hold.

Don't block out your doubts, but examine them well; turn them around in your mind; discuss them with wise and patient friends. Have the courage of your (struggling) convictions. God has somehow outlasted thousands of years of champion doubters, lined up to ask their stumpers; He hasn't heard one yet that He can't answer, and yours probably won't knock Him from His heavenly throne either. But if you hide it under the rug or in the closet with that IRS letter, it will lurk at the back of your mind and breed a whole family of doubts. It will collect interest until it bankrupts your faith.

Don't let that happen. Bring it out into the light and "doubt it out."

DOUBT DEFINES OUR FAITH

When you get a question mark all straightened out, what do you have? An exclamation point, of course! Honest questions lead to powerful declarations.

And Thomas answered and said to Him, "My Lord and my God!"

—John 20:28

It's very difficult for me to read this passage without feeling powerful emotion. It's one of the supreme turning points in all Scripture—perhaps the first ringing declaration of the resurrection's transforming power upon an individual life. The most powerful courtroom testimony is that of a hostile witness. Thomas the skeptic replaces his questions with an exclamation: *my Lord and my God!*

I know we'd all like to have been there to see the wonder and worship shining from his eyes. I know we would join him in falling on our knees to worship the conquering King.

Thankfully, we have plenty of opportunity to keep the faith in the midst of our own doubts.

DISARMING YOUR DOUBTS

Confront your doubts head-on, as Thomas did. But you'll want to handle them carefully. Let's discover how you can disarm them.

ADMIT YOUR DOUBTS PERSONALLY

Has this ever happened to you? Sliding into a pew, late for church, you feel tired, edgy, and possibly coming down with a cold. Across the sanctuary, people are standing and testifying: "I won five more souls to the kingdom of God," somebody says. "And I bet some of you have won more souls than that!

I don't know about you, but I feel God's sweet presence every moment of every day." Everyone around you is laughing, applauding, and saying, "Amen!"

Won five souls to the Lord? You can't even enter the church parking lot without honking your horn at someone who got your space. You'd like to stand up and give your testimony. "Hello, everybody. Let me tell you about my week. I haven't felt anything but a lousy sinus headache and a bushel of doubts. I haven't had the sense of God in my life for a long time. I'm barely getting by at work, my family life is in chaos, and to be absolutely honest with you, I haven't seen God doing much of anything." Then you would sit down, knowing not to expect many amens—just the kind of awed stares usually reserved for gorillas at the zoo; perhaps the same glances that Thomas got in that disciple-filled room.

But it would be far better for you to stand up and spill it in public than to smother your tangled emotions in sanitary smiles for months and years. If you're going to make it through the bad times and finally encounter the true goodness of God, you must begin with honesty. You must admit to yourself that it's not well with your soul.

ARTICULATE YOUR DOUBTS CLEARLY

You can't get by with a simple, "Oh, I'm just a natural-born doubter, I guess." No, you're going to have to do better than that. You're going to have to crystallize your thinking and put your finger on precisely what it is that's causing your uncertainty. The nameless doubt is the one you'll harbor. Identify it, describe it clearly, and deal with it.

Are you struggling with the historicity of the resurrection? We have excellent source material to recommend. Are you grappling with the problem of evil? Great minds have grappled before you—and they're willing to share their thoughts. Are you wondering if one brand of faith is any different from another? Make a brand comparison.

Articulate what you doubt and why you doubt. What brought this on? What is threatening to knock your world upside down? Was it something someone said, perhaps some scholar or skeptic? Is there something amiss in the realm of your emotions? Clarify these issues; wipe the clouds away.

ACKNOWLEDGE YOUR DOUBTS PRAYERFULLY

Christian writer Mark Littleton found a simple formula I like. It goes this way:

Turn your doubts to questions.
Turn your questions to prayers.
Turn your prayers to God.[1]

You mean we can take our doubts directly to God? Won't He be offended? Not according to scriptural precedent. Consider the case of Gideon:

And the Angel of the LORD appeared to him, and said to him, "The LORD is with you, you mighty man of valor!" Gideon said to Him, "O my lord, if the LORD is with us, why then has all this happened to us? And where are all His miracles which our fathers told us about, saying, 'Did not the LORD bring us up from Egypt?' But now the LORD has forsaken us and delivered us into the hands of the Midianites."

—Judges 6:12–13

Gideon's doubts surfaced in the very presence of an angel. The angel testified that God was present, but Gideon was bold enough to say, "You've got to be kidding me! If God is with us, why has our land been taken over by criminal gangs? If God is with us, where are all these miracles our grandparents were always going on about? From where I'm standing, it looks like God has gone over to the Midianite side."

It must have gotten God's attention because the next voice we hear is not identified as the angel's—the text tells us that God replied personally to Gideon. He can handle our frustration and our questions.

Sarah, the matriarch of the chosen people, had a bit of the same abrasive edge. God promised a child, then seemed to forget all about it for *decades*. Who could blame Sarah for becoming a little on the testy side? She was pushing one hundred. At any rate, she had not only her doubts but also a good laugh in the bargain. In the face of God's promises, she laughed, not realizing that God was present—as, of course, He always is.

If Sarah could laugh, Jeremiah could cry. You may not have read Lamentations for a while, but the "weeping prophet" came head-on at God with tough questions. And God answered them every time.

David, in the psalms, often pointed an angry finger at God and accused Him of desertion.

Job was a man of the widest faith, but he sometimes flirted with the deepest doubts.

The Bible's best and brightest weren't heroes for their lack of doubts; they were heroes for confronting and conquering them.

ANALYZE THE EVIDENCE DILIGENTLY

Why won't we confront our doubts? Because deep down, we're afraid the doubts will win. We think Christianity is somehow weaker than its accusers.

Young people buy into the notion that Darwinian evolution must be a proven commodity, just because the mainstream academic community proclaims it so. But I've watched as creationists and evolutionists debated the issues—and I've never seen the evolutionists win. Few people stop to realize that the theory of evolution is, as theories go, "the new kid on the block"—it has only a century of acceptance under its belt. The idea of a world created by God has always been with us. Our fundamental doctrines provide a strong foundation, built to last not simply through time but for eternity.

The biblical propositions will be here when all the trendy theories of the day have passed away. In the nineteenth century, Friedrich Nietzsche proclaimed, "God is dead." Two hundred years later, God proclaims that Friedrich Nietzsche is dead. That's the way it goes. You don't find flaws in the Word of God; it finds flaws in you.

A lawyer by the name of Frank Morison set out to debunk the crazy idea of Jesus' resurrection once and for all. He examined the historical evidence with all his legal logic and evidential expertise. Morison sifted through every possibility that might account for the disappearance of Jesus' body—and was left with the biblical explanation. In the end, he wrote a book called *Who Moved the Stone?* The only thing it debunked was his skepticism. His book has become the classic apologetic text for the historical resurrection of Jesus Christ. Like Thomas the doubter, Morison brought honest questions and a willingness to investigate. And God moved the stone that was in Morison's heart.

ACCEPT THE LIMITATIONS HUMBLY

There's one other thing we must account for—the limitations of dealing with doubt. In the end, some mysteries linger. If it weren't so, we'd be left with no holiness, no God of transcendence. Faith must ultimately encompass its own degree of mystery.

Accept Your Own Limitations

I blush to admit this, but the older I get and the more I learn, the more I become aware of my own ignorance. Just when I think I'm pretty smart, I look a little closer and discover the limitations of my knowledge. All I have to do is tune in to the Discovery Channel, read the latest on the world of science, or listen to some of the sharp, cyber-slick young people in our church—and I'm quickly and hopelessly left in the dust. That's when I discover I'm an old-fashioned abacus in a computerized world—and if you don't know what an abacus is, I'm probably just showing my age all the more.

In the face of my limitless limitations, all I can do is bow in humility before our awesome God and say, "Lord, You know my deficiency. You know the limited capacity of the hard drive You wired within me. Help me understand that I'll never have all the answers."

Accept the Bible's Limitations

I may be venturing where angels fear to tread here. This is a sensitive topic, and I hope you'll read this section carefully before firing off an angry letter.

I accept the Bible as the inspired Word of God, and I regard every word as true, from the opening of one cover to the closing of the other. You can put me down with the crowd that holds out for plenary verbal inspiration, and I'm proud to take my stand among them. The Bible is my full and total authority.

God's Word has every shred of truth we need for our lives in this world, but it doesn't take on every question. There are many issues that God didn't see fit to cover in His Word. What we *are* given is our spiritual meat and living water, the daily minimum requirements for the children of God. Side issues must wait for another day.

Sometimes we face difficult questions. People come to me and ask, "What does the Bible say about this?" We need to accept the fact that, occasionally, the Bible opts for silence. God has an answer, but we must trust the Spirit and our own sound mind as we make our decisions.

ADJUST TO THE COMPLEXITY OF THE UNIVERSE

The more we learn about this world, the more complexity we discover. Our great-grandparents knew nothing of molecules, of atoms, of whirling electrons. Our children will delve even deeper into wonders as yet unfound. And on the other end, we knew space was infinite—but somehow it seems to keep growing as we learn more.

Today it's possible for astronomers to look through a telescope and see incredible distances across the galaxy—and we're told that their range is only the equivalent of a wet thimble at the edge of an ocean, so vast is our universe. Realizing the rich detail of the microscopic world, and the infinity of the telescopic world, we come to a deeper appreciation of the majesty of God. Finally, in humility, we're content to know that our minds are too small to encompass the wonder of it all.

Therefore we'll have those moments when we look into the stars with our questions and realize the simple answer is that there is no simple answer. We are finite, physical beings with spirits prone to stretch toward the infinite. We seek to know Him. We seek to understand His universe. We seek the answers to all that we see and touch, within and without. But for now we must rest in the sufficiency of what is given. Someday, in a better place, all questions will be accounted for, all tears will be dried, and all doubts will be finally laid to rest.

But for now, we can join hands with Paul to embrace the infinite:

Oh, the depth of the riches both of the wisdom and knowledge of God! How unsearchable are His judgments and His ways past finding out!

"For who has known the mind of the LORD?
Or who has become His counselor?"
"Or who has first given to Him
And it shall be repaid to him?"

> For of Him and through Him and to Him are all things,
> to whom be glory forever.
> —Romans 11:33–36

Or we can stand with Isaiah and hear God's gentle disclaimer:

> "For My thoughts are not your thoughts, nor are your ways
> My ways," says the LORD. "For as the heavens are higher
> than the earth, so are My ways higher than your ways, and
> My thoughts than your thoughts."
> —Isaiah 55:8–9

We'll never have a handle on the nature of God. We'll never find the box that will confine Him. Be thankful we have room for worship, to stretch toward something so much greater than ourselves. What a terrifying world this would be if we human beings, with all our violence and foolishness, represented the highest authority and the wisest counsel this universe had to offer. Instead we're free to be children, happily deferring to a Father who will take care of everything. If need be, we can bring Him our questions and be certain of receiving, if not precisely the answers we expected, then certainly the answers we truly needed all along.

Susan Shelley, who watched two of her children slip away, kept pounding on the doors of heaven, demanding some reply. For three consecutive nights she asked God for some assurance that her little ones had found comfort and caring. On the third night, as she was asking God again, she heard the sound of little footsteps in the hallway. Her two daughters, seven and four, often came and crawled into bed with their parents. But this time the footsteps came to the doorway and stopped— then receded back down the hall.

The next morning, Palm Sunday, Susan found it difficult to awaken Stacey, the older of the two. Stacey was too sleepy. Her mother asked, "You wouldn't happen to know anything about a midnight wanderer who came to the door of our bedroom last night, would you?"

"Oh yes," said Stacey, perking up. "That was me. I came to your room to tell you that God spoke to me, but you were asleep. So I went back to bed."

Susan wanted to know what God had said.

"He said that Mandy and Toby are very busy, that they are preparing our house, and that they are guarding His throne."

A little chill ran down Susan's spine. "How did God say these things?"

"He spoke to my mind," said Stacey simply. "Then when I thought you were asleep I came back to my bed and repeated the words over and over so I could remember to tell you. It seemed like an important message."

Susan didn't know what to think. Was this the answer to her prayer? Could God really have spoken through a seven-year-old? That, of course, is yet *another* question; we never come to the end of them. All that matters is that Susan, from then on, felt no more worries for her two lost little ones. From the mouth of a babe had come words of reassurance and blessing, consistent with all the Bible tells us of the next world. *Her children were busy! They were guarding the throne!* And they were preparing that place where the family would one day be reunited in wholeness and joy.

The grief wasn't dissipated, of course, and the "why" questions endured. But what God supplied was enough—more than enough. With the strength that proceeds from such wisdom, Marshall and Susan dared to keep enlarging their family. A year after Mandy's death they welcomed a little boy into the world. They named the little one Bayly, after a wise Christian well acquainted with grief. He is well; the whole family is well and happy.

Pain lingers in this life, for the Shelleys as for all of us; questions never end, and the race seems long. But God is good. We tell Him what we want, and He gives us what we need. In the end, we can only stand with Thomas, reaching out to handle for ourselves the impenetrable mystery, and whisper,

"MY LORD AND MY GOD!"

CHAPTER 5

THE GIFT OF GRACE

When it comes to famous hymns, there's none more famous than "Amazing Grace." Beloved for generations, the simple tune and powerful lyrics serve as a poignant spark for worship. There may not be a more sublime response to the truth of the gospel than, "Amazing grace, how sweet the sound that saved a wretch like me."

There's one line among those lyrics, however, that used to spark my curiosity: "Through many dangers, toils, and snares I have already come." John Newton was the author of that hymn, and I used to wonder what circumstances in his life might have produced such a phrase.

I say "used to" because I did some research and found out. Let me tell you, his life was quite a story! Many know of Newton's history with the slave trade, which he later despised. But not many are aware of the remarkable number of close encounters he had with death. He wrote that line because he had lived that line.

Consider a few of his highlights:

- At a shooting party, Newton almost killed himself by accidentally firing his shotgun while scrambling up a bank. The bullet singed the edge of his cap, missing his head by a couple of inches.
- During a severe storm at sea, Newton was sent below deck while the man who took his place was washed overboard.
- Similarly, at the last minute, his captain oddly pulled him away from a river trip in Africa. That boat sank; and once again, the man who took Newton's place drowned.
- Newton once tried to go overboard and retrieve his fallen hat. He was so intoxicated at the time that he nearly drowned. Even sober, he couldn't swim. Someone grabbed him and pulled him back.

Brushes with death have a way of making us consider great big questions about life and eternity. Newton's own close calls edged him closer and closer to his conversion experience. He regarded his survival as proof of the hand of Providence sustaining him over and over, when by any human reckoning he should have perished. Salvation meant more than the hope of heaven to him; it was a literal experience that he had many times, and the sum total of it persuaded him that God must have a particular purpose for his life.

Wouldn't you love to be in heaven when John Newton and Paul sit together and exchange war stories? Believe it or not, you would notice that Paul's were even more hair-raising than Newton's. And Paul's days of pursuing Christians were almost dull compared to his life *after* he became a believer. The book of Acts can be read as a kind of Spirit-filled James Bond movie from the first century. The apostle faces death every chapter or two, then he dusts himself off and proceeds to the next calamity.

Here are a few of Paul's action scenes:

- He survived a murder plot by the Jews first and then the Greeks (Acts 9:23, 29).
- He was stoned nearly to death and then dragged out of a city. Left for dead, he later got on his feet and walked to a new city (Acts 14:5, 19–20).
- Having managed to get the entire city of Jerusalem in an uproar, he was dragged from the temple and then pursued by Roman soldiers (Acts 21:30–32).

Even if John Newton talked about shipwrecks, Paul could say, "Been there, done that"—*three* of those, actually. He could talk about arguing the case for his life before rulers. He could tell about being lowered in a basket from an opening in the wall to escape murder.

Perhaps it seems to you that your own life is fairly humdrum; not exactly Hollywood blockbuster material. You can imagine Paul and Newton looking up at you from that heavenly table and saying, "Now, what's *your* story?" And you'd begin to stammer, "W-well, y-you see, I haven't had too many adventures really; I was a tax accountant," or, "I took care of the house."

But wait a minute. Think a little harder. We all have our portion of dangers, toils, and snares—dramatic or less dramatic, it really makes no difference. We've all endured those seasons when it seemed as if the world was thrown upside down, and us along with it.

Have you ever lost a loved one and thought your heart would break? Have you experienced a painful divorce? Have you ever been out of work, unable to pay bills, and not certain what you were going to do in the immediate future? Or how about this one: Have you ever been a parent? If the answer to that one question alone is yes, then you are an authority on dangers, toils, and snares. I know of no parent who hasn't lain awake nights worrying about his or her children for all kinds of reasons.

Trouble is like home. You're either there, coming from it, or on your way back to it. And I'm certain you've had your share of each of these:

Times of *danger* when you've been truly afraid.

Times of *toil* when you labored almost beyond endurance.

Times of *snare* when you've wrestled with temptation—sometimes winning, sometimes losing.

At this point, I'd like to suggest that you stop, put this book down for a few moments, and do some focused thinking. I urge you to make a list of your most important examples from each of Newton's categories.

Your Dangers:

_____

_____

_____

Your Toils:

_____

_____

_____

Your Snares:

_____

_____

_____

Have you made your list? I'm serious about this. We're not in any hurry here. Let's go no further until you've thought carefully about your dangers, toils, and snares.

Got your list in hand? Good. You've reflected deeply at that pressure point where truth meets experience. Now you're in the right frame of mind to experience a blessing, because in the next few pages, Paul is going to offer us a theology of hope in times of crisis. He's going to show us how to keep the faith. If you can hold those personal experiences of yours with one hand and take hold of the Bible's guidance with the other, you'll gain a critical tool that can help you stay strong and stand firm no matter what life may throw your way.

THE REQUIREMENT OF GRACE

But we have this treasure in earthen vessels, that the excellence of the power may be of God and not of us. We are hard-pressed on every side, yet not crushed; we are perplexed, but not in despair; persecuted, but not forsaken; struck down, but not destroyed.

—2 Corinthians 4:7–9

So far in these pages we have explored four obstacles we must overcome in order to keep the faith and continue running the race set before us when the going gets tough. Those obstacles are fear, discouragement, worry, and doubt.

Now, as we move to the second half of this book, I want to highlight four key blessings God provides His people to empower them when life seems to be at its worst. These are four blessings we can receive and use to remain strong in the face of fear, discouragement, worry, doubt, and whatever else may come our way.

The first of those blessings is grace. And I want to start by showing you from Paul's life why grace is a necessary requirement for living the Christian life.

Imagine a business traveler who is constantly on the go from one city to another, his appointment calendar packed. His clients always have some new crisis that he is expected to handle personally. It's one trivial squabble after another, and he's always laboring to make peace between petty factions. His business is thriving, but there are plenty of headaches and no time for rest.

That was life two thousand years ago—at least for the apostle Paul. His business was church planting, and every new church brought new joy and new crises. Since Paul was the founder of so many congregations, he found himself in the middle of one controversy after another. Corinth was a problem church. There always seemed to be disruptions there:

public immorality, divisions, and now a problem with false prophets. Some of them were challenging Paul's authority, and he wrote the letter that we know as 2 Corinthians to defend his credentials and to help the church members think spiritually about the problems they were encountering.

In 2 Corinthians 4:7, we find Paul trying to help his readers see the glory of our heavenly Father in the dust of everyday experience. That's what makes a huge difference in this life: seeing things from God's perspective. Paul was showing that it can be done because God has been revealed in human form through Jesus Christ, the ultimate Treasure in an earthly vessel—flesh and blood. All the eternal and infinite glory of God shined through the humanity of His Son, who was fully human and yet fully divine. Jesus' enemies saw Him as just another man, but behind those eyes dwelt the one true God.

That's certainly a wonderful truth, but what does it have to do with your problems or those of the Corinthians? Here comes the part that should send a chill up your spine, as it does mine. If we are ministers of Christ—and I don't mean paid ministers of a church but the kind of minister every single Christian is by appointment—then we share in that eternal glory. As the Father dwelt in the Son, the Son dwells within us through the Spirit. We have this treasure, the ministry of Christ, in our "earthly vessels," our frail and imperfect human bodies.

This is a difficult concept to understand, but Paul always had a handy word picture available. This time he used the idea of a clay jar. If there was one absolutely ordinary, run-of-the-mill object that everyone in the Middle East could understand, it was a clay jar. Cheap pottery was everywhere and used for everything. The jars were breakable, but it didn't matter because it was so easy to get another one. Clay earthenware was as common as—well, as the clay beneath one's feet.

A clay pot had absolutely no value in itself. Everyone knew that. On the other hand, it could hold a priceless pearl, a gold piece, a bite of bread to fend off hunger, a day's drink of water, a wedding ring, even a sleeping newborn baby. It wasn't the jar but the treasure inside that counted.

I know people who carry Bibles that look as if they've been through several shipwrecks with John Newton. The covers are wrinkled and torn. The pages are nearly falling out. But the worn-out container holds the eternal Word of God.

It's not the vessel but its contents. A lowly clam hides a pearl; a lump of coal compresses into a diamond. We fall for one of the devil's greatest lies when we assume that our human limitations make any difference to the workings of God through us.

There will certainly be problems. Clay has its cracks, its heat limit, its fragility. But it still does the job and holds its precious cargo. "Just think about all that I've gone through," Paul was saying. "Is God any less real because I've been beaten and had rocks thrown at me? No—*more* so to us, because He bears testimony through all these things."

Dangers, toils, and snares. They just come with the territory. Paul told Timothy he might as well expect to be mistreated, because the godly in Christ Jesus are always persecuted (2 Timothy 3:12).

For all these reasons and more, we need His grace.

THE RESOURCE OF GRACE

It happened that Paul was once raised to the heavens by God to see glories no man had ever previously beheld. For the Lord's purposes, this vision was necessary for Paul. On the other hand, so was an infirmity of some kind. Why? Because Paul's supernatural experience would tend to breed pride. It could ruin him for ministry. Therefore, God allowed a "thorn," literally a stake driven into the flesh. And "a messenger of Satan" was allowed to "buffet," or beat, him. In 2 Corinthians 12:7, Paul spoke in language descriptive but not precise. He didn't tell the precise nature of the suffering he endured, but he did tell us all we need to know: trials are allowed by God to help us keep perspective and to enable us to grow spiritually.

It's interesting, isn't it? The greater the Lord's plans for us, the more we generally need to be tried. The more critical an army's mission, the harder the army needs to be drilled. The more significant the lesson you're teaching your children, the more discipline you'll need to employ. We think it strange when James tells us to consider it joy to endure a trial (James 1:2–3), but in truth, nothing could make more sense.

If you're involved in tough times right now, congratulations! God loves you, and He has great things ahead for you. Sometimes His earthen vessels simply need to be heat-treated.

Paul said of his suffering, "Concerning this thing I pleaded with the Lord three times that it might depart from me. And He said to me, 'My grace is sufficient for you, for My strength is made perfect in weakness'" (2 Corinthians 12:8–9).

It's good advice to consider our sufferings a joy, but no one is very good at that. Even Paul asked God to take away his trouble—his thorn—three times. The result? God turned him down three times.

Question: Is there any such thing as an "unanswered prayer"? Or would it be wiser to call them "unwanted answers"?

Yes, there are times when God doesn't give us what we want. But in those cases, He speaks to us in ways that are just as valuable as the thing we prayed for. The question is whether we are listening. In the case of Paul, for example, God gave this answer to the prayer: "My grace is sufficient for you" (v. 9). There is very rich, very practical wisdom in that answer—much more than a blunt "no."

It's as if God is saying to us, "I will not take away the trial, but I will give you the power to endure it." Here's another way of putting it: "I won't give you what you want, but I'll give you what you need in order to keep the faith. If I took away the trial, you would grow no stronger—in fact, you would be just a little weaker and more helpless, like a pampered child. But if I allow the trial and help you endure it, you will be stronger, wiser, and more useful to Me."

Another long truth in God's short answer: there is power in the grace of God. The verb translated "is sufficient" is in the present tense—as is God's grace, which is always present. In every situation, we can rely on Him to provide strength and courage. He will never give us all that we want, but He will always give us all that we need.

Compare our Lord to the gods of all the world's religions and you'll find that grace is the difference maker. It is the X factor that radically sets Him apart. Our God is "the God of all grace" (1 Peter 5:10). He is kind, benevolent, and long-suffering. We need not beg Him, bribe Him, or appease Him.

He actually longs to bless us every single moment, every single day. He comes down to us rather than demanding that we climb the impossible ladder to infinity to reach Him. Grace is God taking the initiative.

In this same letter, Paul explained, "God is able to make all grace abound toward you, that you, always having all sufficiency in all things, may have an abundance for every good work" (2 Corinthians 9:8).

Notice the repetition of the word *all*. *All* grace abounds toward us so that we are *all* sufficient in *all* things. He is all we need in all we face, so that for all we do, we can overflow with His grace and power. Did you know it was possible to live like that?

One Friday morning, British pastor Charles Haddon Spurgeon was challenging his ministerial students. He said:

There are many passages of Scripture which you will never understand until some trying experience shall interpret them to you. The other evening I was riding home after a heavy day's work; I was wearied and depressed; and swiftly and suddenly as a lightning flash, this text laid hold on me: "My grace is sufficient for you!" When I got home, I looked it up in the original, and finally it dawned upon me what the text was saying, MY grace is sufficient for THEE. "Why," I said to myself, "I should think it is!" and I burst out laughing. It seemed to make unbelief so absurd. It was as though some little fish, being very thirsty, was troubled about drinking the river dry; and Father River said, "Drink away, little fish, my stream is sufficient for you!" Or as if a little mouse in the granaries of Egypt, after seven years of plenty, feared lest it should die of famine, and Joseph said, "Cheer up, little mouse, my granaries are sufficient for you!" Again I imagined a man way up on the mountain saying to himself, "I fear I shall exhaust all the oxygen in the atmosphere." But the earth cries, "Breathe away, O man, and fill your lungs; my atmosphere is sufficient for you!"[1]

Think of it this way. When you have a big problem, ask yourself, "How big is the problem?" Then ask yourself, "How big is God?" I tremendously doubt the time will ever come when you find that the problem is the larger of the two.

Kenneth Wuest says it this way:

There is enough grace in God's heart of love to save and keep saved for time and eternity, every sinner that ever has or ever will live, and then enough left over to save a million more universes full of sinners, were there such, and then some more. There is enough grace available to give every saint constant victory over sin, and then some more. There is enough grace to meet and cope with all the sorrows, heartaches, difficulties, temptations, testings, and trials of human existence, and more added to that. God's salvation is an oversize salvation. It is shock proof, stain proof, unbreakable, all-sufficient. It is equal to every emergency, for it flows from the heart of an infinite God freely bestowed and righteously given through the all-sufficient sacrifice of our Lord on the Cross. Salvation is all of grace. Trust God's grace. It is superabounding grace.[2]

THE RESULTS OF GRACE

We agree that we are just ordinary clay pots to be used to display God's power. We even accept that we will be prodded by painful experiences in order to learn that grace provides all we need. Now the good news! Here's the upshot of our humbling and our thorns—the result of trials is strength to run our race to the end.

Let us consider just a few of the ways God's grace infuses our lives and makes us strong.

THE GRACE OF GOD PRODUCES POWER

And He said to me, "My grace is sufficient for you, for My strength is made perfect in weakness." Therefore most gladly I will rather boast in my infirmities, that the power of Christ may rest upon me. Therefore I take pleasure in infirmities, in reproaches, in needs, in persecutions, in distresses, for Christ's sake. For when I am weak, then I am strong.

—2 Corinthians 12:9–10

Paul hated the thorn that plagued him. But in time, he accepted it. He knew there could be no ministry if there were no trial because this life wasn't about Paul's strength but God's. The weaker Paul appeared, the greater the Lord would be glorified.

Let me ask you: If you were the most talented person in the world, would that help or hinder your witness? People would say, "You can believe what you want when you have that much natural ability." But when we see absolutely ordinary individuals change the world for Christ—and our history is absolutely filled with those—we can have no doubt of the presence of God in this world.

The next time you think it's all about your strength or talents, remember the following:

- God used an uneducated fisherman to be the church's first great leader. His name was Peter.
- God used a fix-it man sitting in jail to write *The Pilgrim's Progress*, one of the greatest classics in the English language. His name was John Bunyan.
- God used a shy, obscure monk to set off the greatest Christian reformation in history. His name was Martin Luther.
- God used a Bible college dropout to preach the gospel to more people than anyone in history. His name was Billy Graham.
- God used an ordinary shoe salesman to create revivals and new ministries all over the world. His name was Dwight L. Moody.

It was Moody who said, "If this world is going to be reached, I am convinced that it must be done by men and women of average talent." The story is told of an occasion when he was preaching in London. Members of the royal family and other VIPs were present. When Moody came to the name Eliseus in Luke 4:27 (KJV), he couldn't seem to get the word out of his mouth. He began reading the verse again from the beginning, but he still stammered over the E word. A third time: same results. Deeply troubled, he closed his Bible and said, "Oh, God, use this stammering tongue to preach Christ crucified to these people." From that moment he preached with a power his closest followers had never heard. The crowd was awed by the presence of God that evening.[3]

This is among the deepest of spiritual truths. Remember that the ultimate treasure in an earthly vessel is God's own Son, whom the establishment believed it could kill. Because He was composed of flesh and bone, they assumed He was simply one more man who could be squashed beneath the thumb of the Roman Empire. He was simply a peasant carpenter from Nazareth, or so they thought.

What if God had chosen instead to save the world as His chosen people wanted it saved, through the military genius of a fabulous leader? What would that say of God, if anything at all?

Instead, countless people have come to Christ through concluding that only one kind of power could possibly turn the world upside down as it did within decades. The weakness of humanity is the proper container to glorify God.

THE GRACE OF GOD PROVIDES PERSPECTIVE

> For our light affliction, which is but for a moment, is working for us a far more exceeding and eternal weight of glory, while we do not look at the things which are seen, but at the things which are not seen. For the things which are seen are temporary, but the things which are not seen are eternal.
>
> —2 Corinthians 4:17–18

When you struggle with some trial, your first question might be, "Why is this happening?" A better one would be, "What is God teaching me?"

It's difficult for us to remember that God's great desire is for us to see things as they really are, rather than as they appear to be. As Paul said, we see in a mirror dimly right now. God is always working to remove the fog so that we might share His heavenly perspective. Have you ever met a child who was given her every desire? What is the result of that kind of parenting? It creates spoiled, undisciplined children who believe the world will always serve their requests on a silver platter when they snap their fingers.

I'm sure you'll agree good parents don't raise their children that way. Instead, they deny their children certain demands when it is appropriate to do so. Effective parents are always using the moment for an object lesson. They let their children know that love is not the same as pampering. Would your Father in heaven be any less wise in His parenting? He refuses to solve all our problems, but He gives us all the sustaining grace we need for toughing it out.

Can you remember taking your child to a new Sunday school class when she was three years old? She may have cried. She may have clung to your legs and begged you not to desert her until the situation tugged at your heart. You may have experienced every impulse to simply give in and take your child to the adult class with you or stay with her in the child's class. You would have then failed to help your child learn how to adjust to a new environment. Instead, you would have taught her that a pathetic demeanor will manipulate desired results.

Now consider that time when you were in an adult-sized version of that situation: you were unemployed or grieving over a lost relationship, perhaps. As you cried out to God, don't you think it tugged at His loving heart? Don't you think He longed to gather you up in His arms and give you everything you wanted? But He loved you enough not to give in. He knew how much wiser and stronger you would become through learning to depend upon His grace in a time of storm. Once your pleading was over and you had calmed down—just as the child does in a new Sunday school classroom—you were able to hear God say entirely new things to you. You could feel yourself growing. You said, "I made it through this trial by trusting God, and next time I won't be knocked down so easily."

Let's consider the remarkable ways God nurtures us through our struggles, according to this passage of Scripture.

Afflictions Help Us Anticipate Glory

Reigning with Christ requires suffering with Him—no cross, no crown. But holding the hand of Christ through the darkness gives us a glimpse of the glorious nature of deliverance that is to come.

Light Things Help Us Appreciate Heavy Things

Paul called it "light affliction," and frankly, that's what most of our sufferings are. These are like smaller models of the "higher" suffering called death, and the higher glory of eternal life. God teaches powerful truth through lesser mediums.

Temporary Things Help Us Appropriate Eternal Things

"For the things which are seen are temporary, but the things which are not seen are eternal" (v. 18). The hope of wearing Olympic gold drives athletes to persevere through, and even to value, the pain of dedication. Comparing the value of temporary pleasures with potential glory, they press on. Gold medals are of fleeting value. Some even turn up in pawn shops to be exchanged for a different metal. The goal before us also requires rigorous perseverance through pain. Unlike the hopeful competitor, we can have confidence that every trial, every struggle, has a particular purpose to produce in us some eternal value—provided we keep the faith.

Outward Pain Helps Us Accelerate Inward Progress

"Therefore we do not lose heart. Even though our outward man is perishing, yet the inward man is being renewed day by day" (2 Corinthians 4:16). Isn't it exciting that modern-day science is only now beginning to affirm what the Bible has said all along? There is a close relationship between body, mind, and soul. This is why you've met people with physical challenges who have extra layers of wisdom that few others have attained. Bodily suffering drives us deeper. We find God at the broken places, teaching and encouraging.

John Newton wrote, "We will look back upon the experiences through which the Lord led us and be overwhelmed by adoration and love for Him! We will then see and acknowledge that mercy and goodness directed every step. We shall see that what we once mistakenly called afflictions and misfortune were in reality blessings without which we would not have grown in faith."[4]

We can't wish away our problems, and we're unlikely to put on a fake smile and pretend we're enjoying them. What we can do is meet them squarely and soberly, refusing to view them as random shots from an unkind world. Instead, we know they are necessary challenges for the positive growth we're intent on experiencing. Who wants to remain a child forever? We know we need a good workout. We know it's necessary to build our spiritual muscles. There are no muscles of any kind that strengthen without resistance.

When you're at the gym, sometimes you can get through a grueling cycle on some machine by thinking about the muscles that machine is helping. I suggest you do that very thing during times of struggle. Where can you "feel the burn"? What part of your character is going to be that much more godly tomorrow? My friend, perspective will completely change the way you approach challenges.

In one of his books, my friend Ron Mehl wrote these words.

Storms always leave us with a list of things to clean up and fix. They are times when God restores to us the things we lose through negligence, ignorance, rebellion, or sin. For the Christian, storms are a no-lose proposition. They help us to see and acknowledge the loose shutters, missing shingles, and rotten fence posts in our lives while turning us back to the only One who can make the necessary repairs.[5]

THE GRACE OF GOD PROMOTES PERSEVERANCE

> We are hard-pressed on every side, yet not crushed; we are
> perplexed, but not in despair; persecuted, but not forsaken;
> struck down, but not destroyed.
>
> —2 Corinthians 4:8–9

In 2 Corinthians 6:4–5, Paul listed his personal struggles as tribulations, needs, distresses, stripes, imprisonments, tumults, labors, sleeplessness, and fastings. Remember, his authority was under attack at this church. Consider the fact that he chose his *problems* as his credentials. Can you imagine a pastor offering such problems to a church as his résumé today? Paul suggested sleeplessness and prison time as two of the reasons he would make a good pastor. And, of course, he was right.

Notice also the four gauges Paul used to demonstrate the difference the grace of God made in his life (and will make in yours). Each of these gauges takes some particular measure of the emotional state. Imagine the first gauge. At one end of the gauge is the word *Victorious*; at the other end, *Defeated*. Because of grace, the needle keeps hovering near the victorious end of the meter, and that means that in spite of the pressure, you can keep going. The second gauge shows *Confident* and *Despairing* as the extremes, and while we may often be more perplexed than confident, because of grace, we are never despairing. No need to slow down.

These gauges are the difference between an empty fuel tank and one that is simply low. Grace makes that difference: you proceed with caution, but you're not out of gas on the side of the road. Here are the four gauges:

He Was Pressured but Not Defeated

Paul was saying he felt the pinch, but he wasn't crushed. The term "pressure" means being pushed into a narrow place. Paul was a man who spent time in some very small prison cells. As you know if you've read his prison letters, his joy could not be compacted by lack of space; it only became greater. Grace moved that needle.

He Was Perplexed but Not Despairing

Church problems left Paul at his wit's end sometimes. But he never gave up, and he always found the right answer. Grace kept him moving toward the right solution.

He Was Persecuted but Not Deserted

The word for "persecuted" derives from the idea of being pursued or chased. As we've seen, Paul knew something about that kind of hunting, and he also knew about being hunted. Even when it seemed that his enemies vastly outnumbered his friends, he never felt deserted because almighty God was always with him with sufficient grace for his every need.

He Was Pounded but Not Destroyed

The verb "pounded" here means "to be struck down." Paul was often knocked down, but he was never knocked out. He was sometimes left for dead, but he did not die. He kept getting back up to preach the gospel of God's grace. When he was in prison, his work seemed to flourish. To the very end of his life, he was planning on new destinations and new churches. The kind of hope Paul had cannot be suppressed no matter how you pound it. Grace renders it eternal.

THE GRACE OF GOD PROMOTES PRAISE

Sometimes we can gather hidden jewels simply by taking a closer look at Paul's sentence structure.

For example, notice the three phrases in these passages that begin with the word *that*. It may seem to you like an insignificant word, but Paul actually used it as a bridge from human action to godly destiny. *That* means "in order to" or "so that."

Here are the three statements:

- "That the excellence of the power may be of God and not of us" (2 Corinthians 4:7).
- "That the life of Jesus also may be manifested in our mortal flesh" (2 Corinthians 4:11).
- "That the power of Christ may rest upon me" (2 Corinthians 12:9).

Reading them together, we see a pattern emerge. We do what we do:

- that *God's power* will be present in us.
- that *Jesus' life* may be manifest in us.
- that *Christ's power* may rest upon us.

Again, Paul was pointing us to a bridge that Christ has built. On this side of the river, you experience dangers, toils, and snares. It's so easy to be discouraged and to develop a negative and cynical attitude. Then our friend Paul beckons to us. He points to these bridges that seem to disappear into the fog that lies upon the river. We decide to cross those bridges because things can't be any worse than they are on this side.

On the other side, we find the limitless power of God and the rejuvenating life of Christ.

But what precisely are those bridges? They are *attitudes* about our lives and our trials. The attitudes of the world lead to a dead end. The attitude on these bridges takes us to a whole new world. We realize that there is a purpose to our pain. God is up to something, and it's always something very good, something worth cherishing hope for. We begin to trust, putting our eyes on Him rather than on our struggles. Having done that, we find ourselves walking—one tentative step, then another. We hear the echo of our footsteps beneath us on the bridge. We move into that mist. And then we begin to make out the shapes that lie on the other side: shapes of maturity, of wisdom, of new strength and new service for God.

Before we know it, we're not thinking of our infirmities at all. We realize we have what we need. We can keep the faith.

John Newton experienced great loss on this side of the bridge. He had hoped, with all his heart, that he would precede his wife to the grave. But it became clear that his beloved Mary was growing weaker every day. This was surely the ultimate test of his faith, for he had an abiding love for her after many years of marriage. Having been married for twenty-two years, he wrote her a letter that said, "Every room where you are not present looks unfurnished."[6]

But one day he was confronted with the prospect of living out his life in unfurnished rooms. Newton's friends worried about him; they couldn't imagine how he would handle life without Mary by his side. The Christian should be hard-pressed, yet not crushed; perplexed, but not in despair. Would Newton have that demanding level of spiritual maturity?

On the day of Mary's death, Newton preached at the regular service time. The next day he visited parishioners, and finally he preached the sermon at her funeral. Did he grieve? Of course he did—powerfully. He later wrote,

> The Bank of England is too poor to compensate for such a loss as mine. But the Lord, the all-sufficient God, speaks, and it is done. Let those who know Him, and trust Him, be of good courage. He can give them strength according to their day. He can increase their strength as their trials increase . . . and what He can do He has promised that He will do.[7]

Newton had tried that bridge and found it would bear his weight. As a matter of fact, the grace of God has limitless strength. Every single one of us can trust our very lives to it. It has never failed, and it never will.

His grace is sufficient, no matter what we may be facing right now. His grace will lead us through every trial imaginable until we begin to look upon one another and see not ourselves but the image of Christ Himself, our hope, our refuge, and our goal. On that day, you and I will look back upon these earthly anxieties with hearts of loving gratitude. Troubles are very real, but in the light of His presence, they somehow fade into the mist.

CHAPTER 6

THE POWER OF PERSEVERANCE

At the 1983 Australian Ultramarathon—a footrace of 544 grueling miles from Sydney to Melbourne—an odd competitor showed up. Everyone else was a highly trained, commercially sponsored professional. But Cliff Young was a sixty-one-year-old farmer. Unlike the others, who were clad in professional running shoes and cool athletic gear with sponsored logos, Cliff wore a loose white shirt flopping over baggy overalls. He had rubber galoshes over his boots and a white baseball cap hung with sun-screening flaps.

The officials laughed, thinking they were being set up for a joke. But Cliff was serious and ready to run. His name went down on the roster, and someone pinned a number on his faded overalls. Uncertainty about Cliff continued as the runners lined up to start the race. Was this old man really going to compete against young, highly trained athletes with sculpted bodies? Some still thought it was a joke. Others thought him naive or perhaps a little deranged. Some jeered and shouted insults.

When the starting gun fired, the runners took off. The crowd laughed at the contrast between the young contestants' disciplined strides and Cliff's odd-gaited shuffle. But five days, fifteen hours, and four minutes later, no one was laughing. Cliff Young crossed the Melbourne finish line almost ten hours ahead of the second-place runner. The astounded press descended on him en masse. How did this aging farmer accomplish such a spectacular run?

Two facts emerged: First, as a shepherd too poor to own a horse, Cliff often herded entire flocks of sheep alone, sometimes running day and night to keep up with the flock. Second, he didn't realize that runners in ultramarathons stopped at night to rest. He had run the entire distance without sleeping.[1]

Cliff Young had the primary attribute required to win any long-distance race: perseverance. He just kept on going. While his competitors eased their ordeal with rest, he relentlessly pushed through his exhaustion. His eyes were on the goal—and nothing else.

Clearly, we need perseverance in order to run the race God has set before us in our lives. We especially need perseverance to keep the faith and keep running when the world feels out of control. Importantly, though, you and I do not need to be the source of that perseverance. In fact, we shouldn't be. We can't run very far or keep going very long on our strength alone.

That's why God gives perseverance to His followers. As we

determine in our minds to keep the faith, He fills us with all that we require to keep going—to keep running.

There is an amazing promise found in the book of 2 Peter that I want to make sure you know about: "His divine power has given us everything we need for a godly life through our knowledge of him who called us by his own glory and goodness" (1:3 NIV). Right there in black and white, God has promised to give you everything you need to live an authentic, impactful life as a member of His kingdom. And one of those things you need is perseverance. Look at what Peter wrote later in that chapter:

> Make every effort to add to your faith goodness; and to goodness, knowledge; and to knowledge, self-control; and to self-control, *perseverance*; and to *perseverance*, godliness; and to godliness, mutual affection; and to mutual affection, love. For if you possess these qualities in increasing measure, they will keep you from being ineffective and unproductive in your knowledge of our Lord Jesus Christ.
>
> —vv. 5–8 NIV, emphasis added

The word *perseverance* literally means "to bear up under." It describes someone who remains steadfast in the face of severe trials, obstacles, and suffering.[2] Perseverance is a never-give-up attitude, a commitment to move forward when everything is conspiring to hold you back. No matter what happens, you finish the job. Think of the English word itself: *persevere*. The prefix *per* conveys the idea of "through," so perseverance is the ability to go through a severe time.

Perseverance turns ordeals into opportunities. It gives us

the opportunity to finish what we begin, to outlast pain and sorrow, to strive until we accomplish things that are difficult, and to demonstrate God's grace in all the seasons of life.

As Eugene Peterson wrote,

Perseverance is not resignation, putting up with things the way they are, staying in the same old rut year after year after year, or being a doormat for people to wipe their feet on. Endurance is not a desperate hanging on but a traveling from strength to strength. . . . Perseverance is triumphant and alive.[3]

THE FORCE OF PERSEVERING

Those who learn to accept and use God's gift of perseverance are forces to be reckoned with. In a world where most people give up and give out, those who keep going will accomplish more than they can imagine.

In Luke 8, Jesus told a parable about four different soils. The sower threw out his seed, and some of it, Jesus said, fell on good soil where it germinated. Jesus was actually speaking about the heart of someone who embraced the gospel message. Notice the way He put it: He said the good soil "stands for those with a noble and good heart, who hear the word, retain it, and *by persevering* produce a crop" (v. 15 NIV, emphasis added).

Perseverance has the power to accomplish a remarkable harvest through the person possessing it. It adds forcefulness and fortitude to our personalities, and it enables us to reap the harvest, gain the victory, finish the race, and glorify the Lord.

Byron Janis, a world-class concert pianist, played with the world's top orchestras and recorded many albums. From early childhood he studied with elite teachers and practiced for hours every day. Audiences marveled at the grace and nimbleness of his fingers as they flew across the keyboard, bringing to life the classical repertoire's most difficult pieces.

In 1973, at the peak of his career, Janis noticed a creeping stiffness in his fingers. After several tests, doctors gave him the devastating diagnosis: he had severe psoriatic arthritis in both hands and wrists. The prognosis was bleak. His fingers would become stiff as wood and severely crippled.

When arthritis fused joints in nine of his fingers, it appeared his concert career was over. But Janis was determined to challenge this. Without revealing his disease to the public, he spent long hours adapting his playing technique to this new reality. He relied on regular medications, acupuncture, ultrasound, and even tried hypnosis to cope with the pain. His wife, Maria, learned and applied a therapeutic massage technique to restore flexibility to his joints.

Janis continued playing for twelve more years, keeping the state of his health private. The world learned of his condition when he disclosed it at a 1985 White House concert. Despite several more surgeries on his hands, Janis continued to play the piano and became an active fundraiser for the Arthritis Foundation. He credits hope and perseverance for his success in overcoming his severe trial. As he put it, "I have arthritis, but it does not have me."[4]

In this fallen world, trials and suffering are inescapable. And they don't go away when we become Christians. The good news is perseverance can transform our curses into blessings. As Janis said in an interview, "Arthritis has taught me to look inside myself for new sources of strength and creativity. It has given my life a new intensity."[5] In other words, it made Byron Janis a force to be reckoned with.

Receiving God's gift of perseverance has more benefits than you can imagine, but the impact can be summarized in two broad categories.

PERSEVERANCE PRODUCES TRUST

The Old Testament patriarch Job is probably history's best-known sufferer. For much of his life, he was an exemplary, godly man with extravagant wealth and a large family. That all changed one day when Satan targeted him for attack. In a series of mind-numbing disasters, Satan destroyed his wealth, servants, and children—all in a single day. Then the devil struck Job with a painful and disfiguring disease. Job was reduced to groveling in ashes and scraping his sores with a pottery shard. His friends came to analyze his problems, but they did more harm than good.

Despite all this, Job never gave up. He maintained his trust in God, who showed up at the end of the book out of a whirlwind and restored Job to a place of unparalleled blessing. Job persevered through forty chapters of suffering, then Job 42:12 says, "Now the LORD blessed the latter days of Job more than his beginning."

The New Testament writer James said, "As you know, we count as blessed those who have persevered. You have heard of Job's perseverance and have seen what the Lord finally brought about. The Lord is full of compassion and mercy" (James 5:11 NIV).

God rewarded Job's perseverance and gave him double of everything he had before. The restoration of Job's wealth and family was the obvious blessing, but I believe there was another blessing that was perhaps even greater.

Job learned that the God who is big enough to control all facets of the universe is certainly able to direct the paths of His people. As Job confessed at the end of his story, "I know that You can do everything, and that no purpose of Yours can be withheld from You" (42:2). He learned to trust in God rather than question Him.

That, my friend, is an enormous blessing.

Perseverance is our willingness to wait on God to apply His grace to our frustrations and His answers to our questions. And as we wait, we continue to move forward. This is no easy lesson to learn, but the relief of learning it is one of life's greatest comforts.

In her book *You Are Not Alone*, Dena Yohe wrote about the pain of dealing with a suicidal, addicted, depressed, and self-harming daughter. Her book has been an enormous help to many worried parents because she's very honest about the prolonged pain of having a child in crisis. One of the hardest things is realizing "this journey might not be over quickly."

Dena said, "How I hoped it would, but lowering expectations helped me to be more patient with the process, especially when we experienced setbacks." But, she said, she found great comfort in repeating a simple phrase: *I can't. God can. I think I'll let Him.*[6]

A lot of tough non-Christians have tenacity and resilience, and we admire them for that. But the kind of perseverance the Bible advocates is possible only with God—it is accessible only through God. We have to wait on Him and give Him time to work His will into our situations. We keep going because when we can't, He can—and we should let Him. Doing so leaves a legacy long remembered.

PERSEVERANCE PRODUCES TRANSFORMATION

The second force that enters our lives through perseverance involves the transformation of our character. As we press forward, we learn so much along the way. In fact, the Bible teaches in both Romans and James that perseverance is at the heart of a mature personality.

Romans 5:3–4 tells us to rejoice in our sufferings, "because we know that suffering produces perseverance; perseverance, character; and character, hope" (NIV).

The book of James echoes that insight, saying, "Consider it pure joy, my brothers and sisters, whenever you face trials of many kinds, because you know that the testing of your faith produces perseverance. Let perseverance finish its work so that you may be mature and complete, not lacking anything" (1:2–4 NIV).

In other words, perseverance is the essence of maturity. If you can't persevere, you won't mature. We face trials because God wants us to learn to trust Him and to press on with grit and grace—that's perseverance.

Spiritual transformation doesn't just happen. It's forged through the fire of difficulty. When we maintain our trust in God despite difficulty or disaster—even when it seems as if the world is on its head—doing so produces a strength of conviction, ethics, courage, and rectitude that Paul summed up in Romans 5 as *character.*

History records many examples of people deliberately inflicting pain on themselves to achieve character. Medieval penitents whipped themselves or wore nail-studded devices that punctured their skin. Certain tribes of Native Americans suspended their warriors by hooks inserted into their pectoral muscles. Eastern mystics walked barefoot over hot coals.

But here's a secret I've learned over my lifetime: you don't need to go searching for trials! The world is well-stocked with an abundant supply. If yours haven't arrived yet, be patient. They're on the way. And when those tough circumstances assail you, don't run or hide from reality. Instead, face them head-on. Persevere through them, and you'll experience the mercy and compassion of the Lord, which will form in you strength of character and a heart that hopes.

Chris Tiegreen wrote,

Technological advancement has made travel, communication, and daily chores incredibly time-efficient, if not instantaneous. The result is that we're not trained in perseverance. We're not accustomed to pains that can't be relieved and problems that can't be corrected. When they come, we send up prayers with almost the same expectation as when we press the buttons on our microwave. A few seconds, we think, and we should be done with it. God usually doesn't work that way. He is thorough and precise, and He will not be rushed. When He tries us in the fire, as He did Job, nothing can get us out. The time cannot be shortened and our growth cannot come more quickly. We must learn perseverance.

Tiegreen continued, "No one has ever become a true disciple without perseverance."[7]

THE FORMULA FOR PERSEVERING

God knows we need trials to form character, just as athletes need resistance to tone their muscles. In His relentless pursuit of us, He will not leave us in our comfort zones, where our spiritual muscles atrophy from lack of use. Instead, He exposes us to obstacles to strengthen our faith, humble our hearts, and refine our character. That's why Paul urged Timothy to "pursue righteousness and a godly life, along with faith, love, perseverance, and gentleness" (1 Timothy 6:11 NLT).

So, how do you receive God's gift of perseverance? How do you find the strength to press on when you feel like giving up? The next time you're close to giving up, consider these biblical strategies for moving forward.

PUT YOUR PROBLEM IN PERSPECTIVE

On a rainy night in 1976, six-year-old Omee Thao and her siblings were awakened by their mother. "They are here," she whispered, "and we need to go now!" Communists had invaded Laos the previous year, and Laotian Christians were no longer safe. Now the soldiers had reached Omee's village. With no time to pack food or water, Omee's family and others crept stealthily to the outskirts of the city, where guides waited to escort them to Thailand.

They slogged through nights of torrential rain, the flooded and muddy trail making travel difficult and miserable. In daylight, they hid under bushes from searching soldiers. They survived on roots and rainwater. Poorly shod or barefoot, their feet were bruised and bleeding. Days later, they began finding the bones of earlier refugees who died trying to flee.

After twelve grueling days, Omee and her family reached the Thailand border. An official attempted to extort money from Omee's mother and clubbed her to the ground because she had none. They were trucked to a refugee camp and herded with other refugees into a space the size of a jail cell. Their meager rations consisted of rice and fish. Several refugees starved to death.

Yet, despite these ordeals, Omee later wrote, "We rejoiced daily and, as followers of Jesus, thanked God for His protection over our lives. Despite the hardship, we knew we had to keep persevering and enduring, for we had the hope that others did not have."

After enduring the camp for two years, Omee's family received a letter from a relative who had reached the United States, offering to sponsor them for immigration. In 1979, they were flown to Appleton, Wisconsin. Life in America was hard at first, but Omee and her family had the perspective of the terrible ordeals they endured. They adapted and finally achieved lives of peace and prosperity.

Omee earned a master's degree from Denver Seminary in 2015 and now serves in church ministry with her husband.

As she wrote, "All the hardships I faced in Laos and Thailand God faithfully turned into blessings."[8]

The Bible tells you to look at your problems in light of eternity. In the book of Romans, Paul wrote: "I consider that the sufferings of this present time are not worthy to be compared with the glory which shall be revealed in us" (8:18). Architects tell us no building is large or small except by comparison to something else. Comparison is the key to Paul's attitude. Putting things in perspective, Paul realized he was trading temporary sufferings for massive, eternally enduring, perpetual joy and delight.

When you weigh the outcome against the cost of your perseverance, not only does perseverance become your first response; it comes to you more *easily*. The current ordeal may wear down your body, but that body will wear down anyway through age. So the choice is yours how to proceed—and I don't know about you, but I'd rather burn out than rust out.

I've mentioned Joni Eareckson Tada in many of my books because her insights as a long-term quadriplegic have inspired me and millions of others. In one of her books, she wrote:

> Looking down on my problems from heaven's perspective, trials looked extraordinarily different. When viewed from its own level, my paralysis seemed like a huge, impassable wall, but when viewed from above, the wall appeared as a thin line, something that could be overcome. It was, I discovered with delight, a bird's-eye view. It was the view of Isaiah 40:31: "Those who hope in the LORD will renew their strength. They will soar on wings like eagles; they will run and not be faint" (NIV).[9]

If you want to keep moving forward, learn to think of your problems from God's perspective. Instead of comparing your challenges to your own resources, compare them to God's great power, His eternal plan, and His divine love. See them against His infinite grace. The trials that seem so large to us are well within His ability to manage, bless, and redeem for good.

JUST TACKLE TODAY

Remember, God will provide the perseverance you need. Your job is to keep putting one foot in front of the other. Tackle life step-by-step. When God appointed Joshua as leader of the Israelites and gave him responsibility for leading them across the River Jordan and conquering the promised land, He told him, "I will give you every place where you set your foot" (Joshua 1:3 NIV). In other words, you can't make any progress unless you go forward one step at a time, but every single step will be a victory.

You don't have to conquer your whole problem at once, nor do you need to accomplish your life's work in one day. God's plan is step-by-step, and you have to take life day by day.

Remember what Jesus said in the Sermon on the Mount: "Seek first the kingdom of God and His righteousness, and all these things shall be added to you. Therefore do not worry about tomorrow, for tomorrow will worry about its own things" (Matthew 6:33–34).

Listen to that! Your worry doesn't help, so just tackle today. God alone is in charge of tomorrow.

People in addiction recovery groups, twelve-step groups, or support groups dealing with grief and other issues know the phrase *one day at a time*. There really is no other way to persevere.

Gerri Willis is a journalist with the Fox Business Network. In the middle of her career, she was diagnosed with breast cancer, and at first she couldn't face the diagnosis. She reached out to one of her colleagues, Jennifer Griffin, who had beaten triple-negative breast cancer. Jennifer told her, "Prepare yourself for the long haul."

In other words, get ready to persevere—to go through severe circumstances.

Gerri's experiences with treatment left her "horrified, shaking like a leaf." But she wouldn't give up. In 2017, she wrote an article about the benefits she's gained through her experience. "No lesson was more important than this," she wrote. "I learned to take life day by day and hour by hour."[10]

I've battled cancer, too, and had many other problems in life. I want to tell you from my heart that if you're going through a difficult personal trial, the words of Jesus contain great power: "Do not worry about tomorrow." Just take things day by day, hour by hour, moment by moment, and step-by-step. Put one foot in front of the other and keep going. The Lord will be with you, and He will secure every place where the sole of your foot treads. He will open up the future for you, and He'll get you there in His good timing.

Just tackle today with Him.

SURROUND YOURSELF WITH ENCOURAGERS

Peter Rosenberger has been caring for his disabled wife for many years, and his ministry to other caregivers has been of great help to thousands. In his book *Hope for the Caregiver*,

Rosenberger pointed out that loneliness is the first thing that, in God's eyes, was not good. Yet many people who are caregivers become isolated. "Regardless of the reasons, time has a way of filtering relationships, and the caregiver is left to fend alone without meaningful interaction outside of a bleak situation that, at best, stays the same for long stretches."

Rosenberger wrote, "There are many reasons for the isolation that caregivers feel, but the results are universally negative. Without positive human connections, everyone suffers."[11]

That's why the phrase *one another* occurs nearly eighty times in the New Testament. If you're going to get through a prolonged struggle, you've got to have some positive supporters to cheer you on, to pray for you, and to brighten the corner where you are currently residing.

When Julie and Dan McConnel learned they would be parents of twins with Down syndrome, they were afraid. Julie was forty-five years old, and the couple already had four children. They faced a trial they had not bargained for. They had no idea how to raise children with Down syndrome. What challenges would they face? What special needs would have to be met? Could they cope with the heavy responsibility? As Julie said, "You feel like you've lost the future you imagined you were going to have." They even considered avoiding the challenge by putting the babies up for adoption.

Seeking encouragement as they prepared for the births, the McConnels connected with other parents of children with Down syndrome through the internet and a local Down syndrome association. These connections paid off. Other families offered much-needed encouragement and advice, particularly a Scottish family who also had twins with Down syndrome.

Greatly reassured, the McConnels abandoned thoughts of adoption. If this difficulty was to be placed on them, they would bear it and persevere.

When Charlie and Milo were born, all doubts evaporated. The McConnels fell in love with the delightful little twins, and there was no looking back, no regrets. Yes, life was more difficult. There were special medications, regular tests, and the twins' learning processes were slower and required more patience. But as Julie said, "You feel like this thing that's the biggest blow you've ever received in your life has suddenly become a tremendous blessing that you're so grateful for. . . . I have these children who are so remarkable and so unique and so special. I feel like I have them for a purpose."[12]

The credo of the modern age is, "I stand alone. I don't need anyone. I have within myself everything I need to make it in this world." But this isn't true. It never has been. As the McConnels drew strength and encouragement from others, so do we all. This is not merely a preference. Having others around us for support and encouragement when the way gets rocky is a real need. It's the fuel that keeps us going.

As Solomon wrote,

> Two are better than one,
> Because they have a good reward for their labor.
> For if they fall, one will lift up his companion.
> But woe to him who is alone when he falls,
> For he has no one to help him up.
> Again, if two lie down together, they will
>   keep warm;
> But how can one be warm alone?

> Though one may be overpowered by another, two
> can withstand him.
> And a threefold cord is not quickly broken.

—Ecclesiastes 4:9–12

KNOW WHEN TO TAKE A BREAK

Another ingredient in the formula for persevering involves taking breaks. Persevering doesn't mean we never rest. Jesus took intervals of rest during His mission on earth. God rested on the seventh day after creating the world and its inhabitants. To rest is one of the Ten Commandments: "Six days you shall do your work, and on the seventh day you shall rest, that your ox and your donkey may rest, and the son of your female servant and the stranger may be refreshed" (Exodus 23:12).

Rest is a principle built into creation. As this passage says, rest is refreshment. It restores the depleted body and mind. How often have you faced a dilemma, desperately needing a solution that would not come? One idea after another enters your head, but none works. Finally, in frustration you lay it all aside and say, "I can't deal with this anymore. I'm going to bed." Then the next morning when you awake the solution comes to your rested mind.

As Anne Lamott said, "Almost everything will work again if you unplug it for a few minutes, including you."[13]

With apologies to ultramarathoner Cliff Young, rest is not a lapse in perseverance. Rest is stopping to take stock, reorganize, and regroup to continue the battle. Rest turns your conscious mind off and enables you to refocus—to see the problem from a new angle.

More importantly, rest indicates trust in God. Overworking yourself to make things happen can mean you trust too much in your own resources. (Remember the mantra of our age—"I stand alone. I don't need anyone. I have everything I need to succeed"?) Your willingness to stop and rest is an expression of your mature trust in God. You can rest because you know He will take care of you.

In Psalm 3, David spoke of how his enemies had increased. But he was not worried. God was his shield, the One who lifted up his head. In the midst of his turmoil, David wrote, "I lay down and slept; I awoke, for the LORD sustained me. I will not be afraid of ten thousands of people who have set themselves against me all around" (vv. 5–6). Despite enemies assailing him, David rested unafraid, knowing God was his strength and protection.

CULTIVATE POSITIVITY ALONG THE WAY

I know there are times when your spirit struggles. But when the opportunity comes for you to laugh or be happy, embrace that moment. You can't be defined by the grimness of any particular situation. You are here to be defined by the reality of Christ in you.

Christians are not stoics who merely endure life with plodding patience. We are Christ-followers who persevere by faith in God's great and precious promises.

More than seven years ago, three firefighters in Wilmington, Delaware, lost their lives in a terrible fire in the Canby Park neighborhood. One of the heroes who perished was a mother, Ardythe Hope. She left behind a precious daughter,

Ardavia, whom the whole Wilmington Fire Department, in effect, adopted.

In 2019 Ardavia was awarded a $25,000 Bridging the Dream scholarship, given to academically successful students who have overcome adversity. She is the first Delaware student to win this award. Her school counselor, who nominated her, said this about Ardavia:

> For everything she's had to deal with, she's one of the most positive people I've ever met. Every day I look forward to see[ing] her. If you didn't know her situation, you would never know it by meeting her. She doesn't carry that, she doesn't dwell on it, she just looks to her future . . . and every day brings a smile and positive attitude to everything she does.

Ardavia also has a message to everyone who has lost a parent. "When it happened to me," she said, "it was a major setback, but I had to persevere. And I just want everyone to know it gets better. . . . I just want everyone to know they're not alone."[14]

You are never alone. Jesus Christ said, "These things I have spoken to you, that in Me you may have peace. In the world you will have tribulation; but be of good cheer, I have overcome the world" (John 16:33).

REFUSE TO QUIT

What if you just refuse to quit? Refusing to quit is the theme of the entire book of Hebrews. The writer was addressing a group of discouraged Hebrew believers, and the key text is in chapter 10: "So do not throw away your confidence; it will be richly rewarded. You need to persevere so that when you have done the will of God, you will receive what he has promised" (vv. 35–36 NIV).

Do you remember what Luke said about Jesus when the time came for Him to leave Galilee and travel toward Jerusalem, where He knew He faced arrest, torture, flogging, and death by crucifixion? Luke 9:51 says, "Now it came to pass, when the time had come for Him to be received up, that He steadfastly set His face to go to Jerusalem."

What remarkable words. Luke seemed to indicate that a look of unconquerable resolution came over our Lord's countenance—an expression that said, "There's no turning back. Let's go and do this."

Hiking the Appalachian Trail has become the lifetime dream for many people, but the two-thousand-plus rugged miles are hard to tackle in one summer. Most hikers who set out from Georgia to Maine never finish, often because of injuries. Jennifer Pharr Davis did it three times. On one hike with her husband, Brew, Jennifer suffered shin splints, hypothermia, and a major illness. Within two weeks of starting, she told her husband she wanted to quit.

"If you really want to quit, that's fine," he said. "But you can't quit now." He told her to eat, rest, take her medicine, and complete at least one more day. By the end of the next day, Jennifer had regained her strength and was ready to press on until she made it all the way.[15]

That's wise advice, isn't it? If you want to quit, that's fine. Just don't do it today. Keep the faith until the sun rises tomorrow.

THE FOCUS OF PERSEVERING

One of the most inspiring scenes of perseverance in recent memory occurred in February 2015 at the Austin Marathon. Among those lined up at the starting line for the 26.2-mile race was Kenya's Hyvon Ngetich, a favorite to win.

She was the leading runner for most of the race until her body began to break down with only two-tenths of a mile to go. She collapsed to the ground, unable to run or even walk. But she refused to give up. As spectators and medical staff cheered her on, Hyvon—with her eyes focused on the goal—crawled inch by inch to the finish line, completing the race in third place.

Afterward, the race director said to her, "You ran the bravest race and crawled the bravest crawl I have ever seen in my life. You have earned much honor."[16]

Another runner, Ramiro Guerra, said, "When you see something like that it's just another reason to say, 'hey, you know what, I'm going to go up and give it my all.'"[17]

As Guerra reminds us, sometimes we need to look at someone else's perseverance to find the motivation for our own. And that brings us to the final secret of this virtue.

We've looked at the force and formula of perseverance; now let's look at its focus. To move forward when you feel like giving up, focus your vision on Jesus Christ, for He is the One who empowers and enables you to keep going. Perhaps the strongest text in the Bible on this subject is Hebrews 12:

Therefore, since we are surrounded by such a great cloud of witnesses, let us throw off everything that hinders and the

sin that so easily entangles. And let us run with perseverance the race marked out for us, fixing our eyes on Jesus,
the pioneer and perfecter of faith. For the joy set before him
he endured the cross, scorning its shame, and sat down at
the right hand of the throne of God. Consider him who
endured such opposition from sinners, so that you will not
grow weary and lose heart.

—vv. 1–3 NIV

The entire ministry of our Savior was plagued with difficulty and opposition. During Jesus' forty-day wilderness
fast, Satan tried to derail Him with temptations disguised
as painless shortcuts to His goal. Throughout His ministry,
He endured opposition, exhaustion, and misunderstanding.
Near the end He vividly foresaw the horrors looming ahead
and prayed in abject agony with sweat pouring from Him
like great drops of blood. Finally, He was falsely accused in a
mock trial, brutally scourged, and nailed to a cross to hang
for six agonizing hours as blood poured from the thorns
lacerating His scalp, from the wounds in His hands and
His back, and finally from the wound of a spear impaling
His side.

And yet He persevered through it all.

The result? Forgiveness for us. The shattering of the gates
of hell. And glorious resurrection from the dead. When we
keep our eyes on Jesus, He gives us the spiritual stamina to
run with perseverance, to endure, and to never grow weary
and lose heart.

When you feel like quitting, just look at the cross. Look at
the empty tomb! Look at His ascension into heaven. Look at

Him there on the throne. Look at His victory. Look at His love for you. Look at His grace. Consider Him. Meditate on Him. Talk to Him. Draw from His Word.

And never give up.

CHAPTER 7

THE ROLE OF RESPONSIBILITY

A few years back, the sports world was subjected to one of the kinds of controversies that now seem so common in modern life. An NBA player named Kyrie Irving posted a link on social media to a movie that many believed to be controversial. I have not seen the film myself, but different news organizations reported that it contains several anti-Semitic tropes. (The film was based on a book that also included those same tropes and several controversial theories.)

As you might expect, just about everybody who knew about that incident had an opinion about it—and chose to express that opinion in as many ways as possible. Many expressed outrage on social media, demanding that Irving be removed from his team at that time, the New Jersey Nets.

Crowds protested the games. Some demanded an apology and a retraction, while others were equally adamant that Irving had done nothing wrong.

It wasn't just laypeople who were interested, of course. The media circus swung into action with various news agencies raining headlines across the internet and entertainment shows venting their anger or frustration nonstop over the airwaves. After several days of this coverage, the Nets decided to suspend Kyrie Irving from playing in games, which of course generated more headlines and more debate. (Somewhat ironically, the movie in question certainly received quite a lot of free publicity because so many people went to such great lengths to express their outrage.)

As I said, all of this has become commonplace in our modern world. It seems like every week is a new opportunity for outrage.

But then something happened that is certainly not commonplace: Kyrie Irving stood up and spoke out. "I am aware of the negative impact of my post towards the Jewish community," he said, "and I take responsibility. I do not believe everything said in the documentary was true or reflects my morals and principles."[1] In addition, both he and the Nets donated $500,000 to the Anti-Defamation League to show the seriousness of their desire to learn and grow.

"I take responsibility." You don't hear those words every day. In fact, it often feels like our culture pushes people to *avoid* responsibility as much as possible.

This can be a natural reaction for us during difficult seasons—during those times when our world gets turned upside down. It's easy for us to react to that difficulty by casting blame as far and wide as possible. We look for every possible reason and every potential excuse to explain why things are going wrong.

Except, we rarely look in the mirror.

That's why I want to look at another gift God uses to bless us and keep us moving forward when we choose to keep the faith as His children. That gift is personal responsibility, and we're going to explore it through the lens of Ecclesiastes 5.

By the time we get to that section in the book of Ecclesiastes, Solomon had already spent two chapters discussing the emptiness of a life apart from God. Then, in the third chapter, he admitted that even so, the stubborn questions remain. But Solomon stood boldly on the declaration that God has a plan, and that even when it is cloaked in several layers of mystery, it is a good plan—a trustworthy plan.

DON'T BLAME GOD

Author John Killinger tells about the manager of a minor league baseball team who got so frustrated with his center fielder's performance that he jerked him out of the game and played the position himself. The first hard-hit ball that came to the manager took a bad hop and smashed into his mouth. His next play was a high fly ball that he lost in the sun—until it smacked him in the forehead. The third ball that came his way was a hard line drive that flew between his hands and popped him in the eye.

Furious, the manager ran off the field to the dugout, grabbed the center fielder by the shirt and shouted, "You've got center field so messed up, even I can't play it!"[2]

When it comes to the difficult seasons of our lives, God is the subject of more than His share of fingerpointing. A seventeen-year-old accused of burning down a church in Nashville, Indiana, explained at his trial that he took a cigarette lighter to the nearly century-old building because, in his words, "I was angry with God."

One woman, having lost both her husband and son in separate accidents, posted a notice on the internet that declared: "I am ANGRY at God. I am VERY ANGRY!" She dared to say out loud what you and I really feel sometimes. When our world is turned upside down, it's easy to believe that God is the culprit.

God understands our anger, and when we pray, it's a good thing to tell Him what we honestly feel. But sustained bitterness toward the Lord who loves us is irrational and unwise.

In fact, in 1999 the *Journal of Health Psychology* reported an interesting study. Social psychologist Julie Juola-Exline and her team of researchers found a link between anger toward God and anxiety and depression. Those who couldn't get beyond their resentment toward God were more likely to experience problems with negative emotions. The good news, according to Juola-Exline, was that "those who were able to forgive God for a specific, powerful incident reported lower levels of anxiety and depression."[3]

"Forgiving God" is a term I'd rather avoid. It implies that God has done something wrong that requires our pardon. We should underline the statement that by the perfection of His nature, He will not and cannot do wrong. What seems like misdeed is mystery. The important thing to remember is that His love and compassion are perfect, unbroken, and forever.

Just the same, we often blame God for our losses and sorrows. Here in Ecclesiastes 5, Solomon gave us some pointed instruction on how to keep the faith instead.

WALK CAREFULLY BEFORE HIM

Walk prudently when you go to the house of God; and draw near to hear rather than to give the sacrifice of fools, for they do not know that they do evil.

—Ecclesiastes 5:1

Imagine stumbling into the house of God loaded down with a heavy burden. It's the dead weight of all your sorrows. You're certainly bringing them to the right place, but you need to bring them in the right way. When you're overloaded, it's important to watch your step.

We want to lay them carefully at the altar rather than violently at God's feet. That is, we need to give Him the burden, but not the blame. There's a difference. That's why we need to tread carefully in the house of the Lord.

Remember that Solomon was the builder of the temple, the most beautiful building on earth in its day. There had never been such a place to bring God and His children together. It was, in a sense, the one place for heaven on earth. The architects understood that such a place should not be entered carelessly or thoughtlessly—particularly not resentfully.

We must decide which side we're on: Do we honor God as the Lord of life, or not? Do we trust Him in the rough times, or only when it's convenient? Our modern expression "Watch your step!" comes from Solomon's warning: "Walk prudently." Literally, the Hebrew says, "Keep your foot."

You may remember a time when you heard that phrase from your parents. You were angry, and your words were approaching the territory known as *disrespect*, when Mom or Dad said, "Watch your step, young man" or "young lady."

Due respect for parents and for God is a sufficiently urgent issue to be enshrined in the Ten Commandments. Life without boundaries is chaos, and when we treat God as if He is not in control and not loving—when we cut Him down to our size through a petty approach or when we wander outside of the boundaries—we invite chaos into our lives.

When we come into the house of God, we're to draw near to hear, to understand, to learn, and to worship. We're to cultivate an attitude of reverence, expectation, and a holy sense of resignation to His will. Blaming God for our struggles does nothing to alleviate them. But walking carefully before Him will aid our efforts to keep the faith.

TALK CAUTIOUSLY TO HIM

> Do not be rash with your mouth,
> And let not your heart utter anything hastily
>   before God.
> For God is in heaven, and you on earth;
> Therefore let your words be few.
> For a dream comes through much activity,
> And a fool's voice is known by his many words.
>
> —Ecclesiastes 5:2–3

Now that we've walked the walk, we have to talk the talk. We must talk cautiously to God as well as walk cautiously before Him—always keeping in mind that we are speaking from a basis of ignorance.

I think often about the terrible fires that have burned a path through our community in Southern California. We often don't know how such a blaze begins. An electric storm could send a bolt of lightning. Some disturbed individual could engage in a conscious act of arson. A careless person could innocently start a great fire without realizing it.

What about God? Could He start a fire? *Of course.*

Could He also prevent or suppress one? *Yes.*

Could it be that He has done so many times in many places without any human being realizing it? *Yes!* That's something we seldom consider. We see every fire God allows but none that He prevents.

So when we philosophize about God's character based upon our limited observations, we speak from ignorance. On a given day, His intervening hand may have prevented some horrendous act of global terrorism—then five minutes later, a single automobile with a drunk driver crashes, and all who knew the victim are giving God a tongue-lashing.

Nothing illustrates this insight more vividly than a widely watched episode of television's *The West Wing* in which the fictional president, Josiah Bartlet (played by Martin Sheen) lashes out at God. Bartlet, battling multiple sclerosis, is anguished over the death of his longtime secretary in a drunk-driving accident. After attending her funeral in the National Cathedral, he waits until everyone leaves, then orders the doors sealed so that he is alone. Standing before the altar,

Bartlet, a Roman Catholic in the television series, lashes out at God.

"She bought her first car and You hit her with a drunk driver!" shouts Bartlet into the cavernous cathedral. "That's supposed to be funny? Have I displeased You, You feckless thug?"

The angry president then launches into a tirade in Latin. Translated, his words are: "Am I really to believe that these are the acts of a loving God? A just God? A wise God? To hell with your punishments!" Then, in a gesture of contempt, the fictional president lights a cigarette and crushes it on the cathedral floor.[4]

The reaction of viewers was predictable. While some were shocked at Bartlet's anger and blasphemous words, others commended him for his expression of brutal honesty and for representing thousands of people in his anger toward God.

Solomon would feel differently. He reminded us that God knows the time and appointed season of every life. He counts the very hairs on your head, and a sparrow doesn't plummet to earth without His awareness. As Jesus told us, "You are of more value than many sparrows" (Matthew 10:31). Moreover, God knows every implication of every event: positive, negative, or neutral. We live in the goldfish bowl of time and space with all the limitations imposed by that habitation. God is outside that bowl entirely, and He sees past, present, future, and all across every inch of His creation simultaneously. We can't wrap our minds around that one any more than a goldfish can understand a map of your county.

Seeing, hearing, knowing, and planning all things, and

based upon His own mysterious purposes, God governs the affairs of this planet. There will be a time for intervening and a time to refrain from intervening. To feel angry and frustrated is human; but to chastise God is to make a cosmic spectacle of our own folly in the presence of the Alpha and the Omega, the King of kings who loves us so much that He bears the nail marks in His hands, in the presence of the seraphim and cherubim, and all the heavenly realm.

Solomon counseled us to be men and women of few words, for the mark of a fool is his airy gust of reckless speech. Verse 3 is difficult to translate, but Solomon seemed to say that a fool babbles on relentlessly, like a man who has had a busy day and experiences dream after dream all night long. And we do sleep better when we don't dwell on our shortsighted grievances against a loving Father.

DON'T BRIBE GOD

When you make a vow to God, do not delay to pay it;
For He has no pleasure in fools.
Pay what you have vowed—
Better not to vow than to vow and not pay.

Do not let your mouth cause your flesh to sin, nor say before the messenger of God that it was an error. Why should God be angry at your excuse and destroy the work of your hands? For in the multitude of dreams and many words there is also vanity. But fear God.

—Ecclesiastes 5:4–7

As a troubled young man walked through a field in Germany, a terrible electrical storm filled the sky. A lightning bolt struck a nearby tree, and he instantly took it as a sign from God. "Help me," cried the young man, "and I will become a monk." That sudden vow changed the life of Martin Luther.

As mentioned in a previous chapter, another young man, a disreputable character named John Newton, made a similar promise to God in the middle of a deadly storm at sea. "Help me," he prayed, "and I will change my life." Out of that prayer came a gradual transformation that led Newton into the ministry and made him a world-class hymnist, the author of "Amazing Grace."

There are times when God uses a storm or crisis to awaken us, and we make life-changing vows and commitments to Him. The problem is that most of us are quicker to make a commitment than we are to keep it. We live in an age of half-hearted vows and ill-kept promises. If every single person kept the promises they made to God in a pinch, then the world would be swarming with millions of missionaries.

We sometimes call this "foxhole Christianity." It's the ultimate expression of using God. Bargaining with God is an extremely questionable activity, generally one to be avoided. But if you do put yourself on the line, don't even think about not making good, for God is not mocked. What is vowed before Him is *binding*, just as He is bound by His many promises in the Scriptures.

Solomon taught us that vows are serious. They are lasting and, in the eyes of God, not subject to "on second thought" revocations.

I love what David said in the psalms as he thought about a vow he had made to God. "I will go into Your house with burnt offerings; I will pay You my vows, which my lips have uttered and my mouth has spoken when I was in trouble" (Psalm 66:13–14).

We don't know exactly what kind of trouble David was in, but whatever it was, God apparently got him out of it. And in the process, David made a vow to God. Vows were not uncommon in the Old Testament, nor was breaking them. Otherwise, Solomon wouldn't have warned against it, nor would Jesus have commented on it when bringing a spiritual perspective to what had become pharisaical traditions surrounding the Mosaic law (Matthew 5:33–37). But David kept the vow he made to God.

Eva J. Alexander was born to believing parents in Chennai, India, and was born again at age twelve during a Billy Graham meeting. In 1963, she married R. D. Alexander, and the two took positions with the government of India. Eva's job exposed her to the plight of women in her country, and she began speaking out about their status and suffering. For a while, she became so socially active that her spiritual life suffered. Politics became more important than her faith.

But the Lord sent a serious illness that brought her to her knees, where she made a solemn vow before the Lord. As she hovered near death in the hospital, she prayed, "God, if You're real, do not allow me to die. I will serve You."

Eva ultimately recovered from her illness. When she returned home, she began reading her Bible again. Two words in Matthew 21:31 tore through her mind like torpedoes: the words "and harlots." Jesus said, "Tax collectors *and harlots* enter the kingdom of God before *you*" (emphasis added). Our Lord wants to bring *harlots* into His kingdom.

A week later, a nearby pastor told Eva of a prostitute who had run away from the brothels, and he asked Eva to provide a room for her. "I can't," Eva said. "You keep her." Eva had a husband and four children at home, including two teenage sons. But once again the Lord brought Matthew 21:31 to mind, and Eva relented.

Her family was aghast: "What is this? You're turning our house into a brothel!" But their attitudes soon changed, and they accepted this ministry as coming from God. Other girls began showing up, and the Alexander home became a rehabilitation center. Police officers and prisons referred troubled women to Eva, with up to fifteen women living in the Alexander home at any one time. The Alexanders provided medical treatment, job training, and a strong gospel witness.

As a result of her vow made to God when she was near death, Eva started a home for the children of prostitutes. In this home, countless children—ages twelve months to thirteen years—have found refuge. Her husband and children joined her work and, spurred on by that passage in Matthew, they have brought many souls into God's kingdom.[5]

We've seen it throughout church history. A promise to God, honored by the one who made it, can lead to a touch of heaven on earth. But a vow in danger of being broken is an idea that should make us shudder with fear. At this moment, when the flames are at the door, a vow comes easily to the lips; but tomorrow, when a cool rain drives calamity from memory, it's too easy to double-cross God. The soul implications could be far worse than the original danger that brought about the vow.

My recommendation? Keep your mouth shut when your back is to the wall, and keep the faith with God. Then keep on keeping on. That's the only vow He's really looking for.

CHAPTER 8

THE FUNDAMENTALS OF FORTITUDE

I've mentioned already in these pages my battle against cancer many years ago. That was a defining season in my life. Certainly one in which my world was turned upside down— not just once but many times in rapid succession. And certainly one in which I desperately needed every gift my heavenly Father was willing to give so that I could continue pressing forward in my race.

In sharing that story here (briefly, I promise), my goal is not to highlight my struggles. Instead, I want to show how those struggles produced fortitude in me. They helped me develop a strength not only for that moment but one that has allowed me to weather the ups and downs and difficulties of life in every season since.

It all began on an ordinary Monday morning with what should have been a routine checkup. It was still early as I arrived at the Center for Executive Health in La Jolla. The exam got underway at 7:45 A.M. with the interview, and I handled the usual barrage of questions from the nurses armed with their clipboards. Then I was ushered over into another part of the clinic for an EKG stress test. It went smoothly, and I could tell my numbers were good ones.

So far, so good. I smiled with satisfaction as the doctors nodded and made little checks on their notepads. They stroked their chins and admitted that I was in pretty fair shape for a grizzled fifty-three-year-old veteran of life's trenches. Better still, the physical exam was downhill all the way after the EKG. I had been through all this before, and it was easy to tell that I was checking out fine on the remaining tests. The men in the white coats gave me the thumbs-up at every point.

Late in the morning, I was taken to an examining room, where I met the head physician. He asked me to lie face up on the table, and I complied. The doctor began to go over my body from head to toe.

Soon I'll have this whole thing behind me, I thought. *It will feel good to have another successful physical in the books. The white coats will hand me the bill and show me the door. I'll be free to climb into my van, drive back down the highway, and get on with my crowded agenda. And I'll have a little extra spring in my step, knowing that for one more round, I've come out victorious in the battle against time and corruption.*

Those were my thoughts. That's when the bomb fell.

As the doctor probed the left side of my abdomen, he said, "Dr. Jeremiah, you have a mass here in your abdomen that causes me some concern. It feels to me as if your spleen is greatly enlarged."

I felt my heart skip a beat. "What do you think it is?" I asked.

"I can't say," he replied quietly, "until we see a CAT scan of that part of your body."

That's it. Three sentences—a handful of words—brought a crowded, thriving life to a screeching halt. As I sat up and dressed myself, I struggled to absorb the doctor's words. My mind launched into "spin-control" mode, searching for positive angles.

I had my scan late that afternoon in the radiology center across the street and was informed that results would be available the following day. At least the suspense wouldn't be prolonged; within hours I would be given words of comfort—or something else.

I was shell-shocked that afternoon as I went through the motions of the scan and closed out my business with the clinic. I was still in a daze as I made my way back to my home in El Cajon.

How was I going to handle this news bulletin there? This was something I needed to handle carefully—it was, after all, a bomb. I knew that Donna, my wife, planned to leave the next day to visit her mother in New Hampshire. She would be scrambling around the house, packing suitcases and orchestrating last-minute arrangements. She'd have that happy, busy glow about her, energized by the anticipation of her trip.

That's why I decided to keep silent. Why rain on her parade? At this point, everything was preliminary and tentative. I decided to let this evening be a bright one for at least one of us. I refused to ruin a pleasant trip for my loving wife.

So I kept the curtains tightly shut on the black clouds inside me. I smiled and made the best I could of the situation. The next morning, I drove Donna to the airport and watched her plane disappear into the blue, trouble-free sky that still existed for other people. Then I headed to my office, where I sat and watched my telephone, waiting for the call that would reveal my earthly fate. The moments ticked by slowly, and every ring was a false alarm.

Finally that afternoon, I picked up the receiver and heard the doctor's calm voice on the other end of the line. I listened desperately for a victorious affirmation—words about tests that came back negative, about lumps that were less than they seemed. I wanted those words desperately, and I poured out my soul praying for them.

But those words were not available to me. Instead, the doctor's fears were confirmed—I had a mass on my spleen.

The doctor carefully explained to me that three radiologists examined the scan and shared the firm opinion that I had lymphoma, a cancer that attacks the lymphatic system, of which the spleen is the center. We talked for a few minutes, then I returned the receiver to the cradle of the telephone. The most terrible phone call of my life was over. I felt emptiness and despair rising up inside me.

It was Tuesday, the day for the staff meeting at our church—another difficult hurdle in my current state of turmoil. I kept the meeting short, dismissing it after a brief time of prayer. Then I sought out my close friend and staff member

Dr. Ken Nichols and beckoned him into my office. I closed the door carefully, sat down beside him, and shared with him the details of my physical and the prognosis. He was the first person with whom I shared the crisis. We cried, embraced, and prayed. Then we pulled ourselves together and began to think about what to do.

Ken had an idea. He remembered a longtime friend of mine—Dr. Marv Eastlund of Fort Wayne, Indiana. I've known him since I was a pastor there many years ago. Dr. Eastlund is not only a knowledgeable physician, but he is also an experienced sufferer who spent six weeks in Mayo Clinic for a pancreatic disorder.

Ken thought Dr. Eastlund might be able to help, and that sounded good to me. I made the call, and Dr. Eastlund didn't hesitate before issuing a directive: go to Mayo Clinic immediately. My kind friend promised to make a phone call to expedite things for me. In a matter of hours, I had an appointment at the Mayo Clinic.

On Thursday morning of that same week, I boarded a plane heading eastward. I was traveling on business—I was scheduled to speak at rallies in New Hampshire and Maine to support our Turning Point radio ministry. My friends Steve and Susan Caudill were flying with me. The plan was for Donna to meet us in Manchester, New Hampshire, at the first rally. As so often happens with air travel, the connections were perilously tight; we arrived at the rally with just enough time for me to kiss Donna hello and hurry to the platform.

The event was thrilling, and it lifted my spirits. The building was packed with fifteen hundred excited listeners. Several of them gave their hearts to Christ that night, securing their eternal destinies. Just at the time I was having a close encounter with death, these wonderful souls were having their first encounters with eternal life. I shook hands, chatted with folks, and signed books and Bibles until the last of the crowd went home.

On the way back to the hotel, Donna and I stopped for a late dinner. That's where the thrill of the evening wore off. I became pensive over my plate because I knew that the time had come to level with my wife about the week's events.

We found our hotel and settled into the room, unpacking our things and turning down the sheets. Then I sat down on the bed and opened to Donna those dark curtains of my soul. I told her the whole story of three days of despair. When I finished, we cried and prayed and held each other through most of the night.

There, far from our home, on the other side of the continent—there, in a strange hotel—we huddled together to face the most challenging moment of thirty-plus years of marriage.

The rallies came to an end, and Donna and I returned home at last. There were more doctors' examinations and troublesome hours of sorting out insurance questions. Our ministry had begun a new insurance plan at the beginning of October, and that coverage would not extend to a trip to Mayo. It looked as if we'd have to settle for surgery in San Diego. I had a date with the doctors for Tuesday morning at Sharp Hospital, at which time my spleen would be removed.

My condition was no longer a secret; I'd begun to call some of my network of ministry friends around the country. I coveted their prayers. One of these men was Lowell Davey, president of the Bible Broadcasting Network. When I called him and described my situation, he responded without hesitation, "David, you are going to Mayo Clinic! If your insurance will not cover it, I'll raise the money myself." I think you'll understand that by this time, Donna and I were spent.

The emotional roller coaster had left us dizzy and exhausted. I told Lowell that my surgery was scheduled for Tuesday morning at seven forty-five—only five days from then. I set a condition. "If you can get me into Mayo Clinic on Monday morning," I said, "then I'll go."

Two hours later, I received a phone call from a doctor at Mayo Clinic, calling to confirm my appointment at seven forty-five Monday morning. I was astounded, to put it mildly. True friendship is a powerful force for strength and encouragement.

With our minds finally set on a course of action, I began to prepare myself for the weekend. I was scheduled to officiate at a wedding for the daughter of my administrative secretary on Saturday afternoon at three o'clock. Once again, I was mindful of my personal situation casting a pall over someone else's joyful occasion—particularly in the case of a wedding. I asked for the couple to be kept in the dark about my crisis until after the ceremony. This was their once-in-a-lifetime day, and it should be filled with joy.

The next morning, I preached at both services. The Lord once again honored His Word. But this was not just another Sunday for me. Afterward, I told Donna that in twenty-five years of preaching, I'd never felt the presence of the Lord as I did that day. Other preachers know this feeling—at times it was almost as if I were sitting on a pew in the back of my mind, listening to someone else preach. I was deeply aware of Paul's statement, "When I am weak, then I am strong" (2 Corinthians 12:10). I'd never been so weak, and He'd never seemed so strong.

That afternoon, we flew east, this time toward Mayo Clinic. During my first appointment, there were rounds of blood tests, physical examinations, and more questions. Finally I met with the first doctor. She went over the results and confirmed the diagnosis of lymphoma. She also made the arrangements for my next appointment, in the department of hematology.

When she called hematology, she was told that no opening would be available until Thursday. My heart sank. This was Monday! Three days seemed like an eternity, and I had work to do back home. How could we wait here for seventy-two hours? The doctor sensed my desperation. She considered quietly for a minute and finally said, "I know one of the doctors in that department. Let me call him."

The doctor called her friend, and I heard her say into the phone, "He's a pastor from San Diego. His name is David Jeremiah." Then a look of surprise splashed across her face. She put her hand over the mouthpiece and turned to me. "He knows you!" she said. Speaking into the phone, she said, "Does that mean you'll see him this afternoon?"

It did. I was instructed to head right over.

My doctor had been speaking to a colleague named Dr. Thomas Witzig, who had once heard me speak at Moody Founder's Week. Dr. Witzig is a wonderful Christ-follower, and it pleased me greatly to discover that he would be the lead physician. When we sat down to talk, he walked me through the procedures to come during the next few days. Dr. Witzig agreed that surgery was required, and it was scheduled for Tuesday morning at the Methodist Hospital in the Mayo Clinic complex.

That's where I went the next morning. The surgery lasted about two hours and revealed that the lymphoma was centered in the area immediately around my spleen. The surgeons decided to leave the spleen in place; it was actually not as diseased as they had anticipated. This was the first tentatively hopeful medical news we'd received, and you can imagine our gratitude.

The doctors patiently educated Donna and me about my condition. They explained that lymphoma is a treatable form of cancer. There are never any guarantees with this dreaded enemy, but we at least had the possibility for recovery through chemotherapy—and that made hope possible.

We held tightly to that hope. Our spirits basked in the prayers, support, and encouragement of our church family and friends; we fed on their support and felt strengthened for the battle ahead. But in the midst of all the love and affirmation, it was the Lord, "a stronghold in the day of trouble" (Nahum 1:7), who knew the needs of my body and soul most deeply. It was He who walked with me through the valley of the shadow, He who lavished upon me a deeper, more personal experience of His presence than I'd ever known before. As I sought refuge in His Word, I found consolation beyond description for my troubled spirit.

Again and again I was reminded of the words of the apostle Paul. Long ago he was confronted with death and fear, and perhaps he experienced emotions a bit like my own. Paul was so gifted and had a heart eager to minister, yet he was forced to bide his time in a dark prison. I know Paul asked God the same questions I have asked, and I'm grateful he recorded God's answers: "And He said to me, 'My grace is sufficient for you, for My strength is made perfect in weakness.' Therefore most gladly I will rather boast in my infirmities, that the power of Christ may rest upon me" (2 Corinthians 12:9).

God's grace is sufficient—I can tell you it's true.

LIFE IS DIFFICULT

You've had a similar experience, I'm sure. Maybe not cancer, but somewhere along your own path, you've faced circumstances you never expected or wished to encounter. I hope you've found it helpful, as I have, to read encouraging words from fellow strugglers.

Gordon MacDonald is a friend and fellow struggler. His fine book *The Life God Blesses* has ministered to me more richly than I can tell you. Gordon writes with wonderful insight about the methods God uses to bring blessing into the lives of His servants. In one chapter, he coins a term to describe one of those tools. He calls them "disruptive moments." According to Gordon, disruptive moments are "those unanticipated events, most of which one would usually have chosen to avoid had it been possible."[1] He adds, "We don't like disruptive moments; they are too often associated with pain and inconvenience, failure and humiliation. Not that they have to be, but that seems the way of the human condition."[2]

Disruptive moments make it seem as if the world is upside down.

Few of us ever fully grasp that simple but painful biblical truth: the heat of suffering is a refiner's fire, purifying the gold of godly character and wisdom. Wouldn't we rather it be a simpler, more comfortable process? But we know life simply doesn't play out that way. Everything worthy in this world comes at a price.

The Russian writer Aleksandr Solzhenitsyn understood the fullest implications of that idea. The point was driven home for him during long years of solitude and suffering in prison, the price he paid for writing a few words of truth about his government. He knew something of disruptive moments and wrote,

> It was only when I lay there on rotting prison straw that I sensed within myself the first stirrings of good. Gradually it was disclosed to me that the line separating good and evil passes, not through states, nor between classes, nor between political parties either, but right through every human heart, and through all human hearts. . . . So bless you, prison, for having been in my life.[3]

Can I say, "Bless you, prison" about my deepest trials? Can you bless the prisons that loom in the future? It takes a deep spiritual wisdom to cultivate that ability—a profound faith that God loves us and that His purposes are truly right for us.

M. Scott Peck begins his bestseller *The Road Less Traveled* with three simple, indisputable words: "Life is difficult." Who will argue with that? Life *is* difficult.

My cancer diagnosis confirmed Peck's words. It was a profoundly disruptive moment in my life. This was no mere bump in the road; it felt like a gigantic and bottomless pothole. It opened up in my road quite suddenly, with no highway markers to warn me, and I plunged into its darkness. I had not been offered alternate routes or given a vote on the matter.

Life is difficult, and difficulty is the only path to wisdom.

FIVE PRINCIPLES TO REMEMBER

Where are you, traveler? Perhaps you're facing a disruptive moment in your life, one you never could have anticipated. Perhaps your road has led to a divorce, a death, a financial disaster, a physical or mental sickness, or the heartbreak of seeing a fellow traveler wander away from the path. Maybe the bend in your road is something so disappointing and devastating that you can hardly bear to acknowledge it. You could be standing by the side of your path, so overcome by pain that you believe you can't move on.

Please remember this: your crisis is important to God. Could it be that you're looking at it from your own perspective? That's not the way our Father behaves toward us. Whatever struggle or setback you face is intended to empower and purify you. Your situation is important to Him because He is using it to make you a more valuable servant in His kingdom.

Let me remind you that your disruptive moments have strengthened you, whether you realize it or not. They have blessed you with fortitude—with the ability to handle bumpy roads in addition to smooth. I know it hasn't been easy, but God has used those difficulties to equip you so that you can continue your race no matter what obstacles may appear in your path.

Having lived through some very disruptive moments of my own, I want to give you five principles to remember as you continue keeping the faith. They've helped me, and I trust they'll be just as valuable in your own travels down that long and winding road.

PRINCIPLE #1: DISRUPTIVE MOMENTS ARE OFTEN DIVINE APPOINTMENTS

Second Corinthians 12 identifies the thorn as Satan's messenger sent to test and torment Paul. But the devil wasn't given free rein; he couldn't do anything to Paul that God wouldn't allow. Remember Job? Satan was allowed to test him, but only with the permission and conditions prescribed by God. Paul and Job always remembered that God was ultimately in control.

The Father is the One who disciplines His children—Hebrews 12 makes that very clear. Every trial we face, difficult as it may be, comes from the hand of God, who loves us and wants us to grow. If we're wise enough, we will see that disruptive moments are really divine appointments.

That perspective will make all the difference for you. It will keep you from lashing out at God in despair. It will keep you from giving in to discouragement. You will say, "God, You are in control—You have a plan, and that's why You have allowed this to happen in my life."

Some years ago I was given a copy of a letter that I can imagine being written by God to someone going through a disruptive moment. It remains as poignant and pertinent now as it did then.

My child, I have a message for you today; let Me whisper it in your ear, that it may gild with glory any storm clouds which may arise, and smooth the rough places upon which you may have to tread. It is short—only five words—but let them sink into your inmost soul; use them as a pillow upon which to rest your weary head:

THIS THING IS FROM ME.

Have you ever thought of it, that all that concerns you, concerns Me, too? For "he that touches you, touches the apple of His eye" (Zechariah 2:8).

I would have you learn, when temptations assail you, and the "enemy comes in like a flood," that this thing is from Me; that your weakness needs My might, and your safety lies in letting Me fight for you.

You are very "precious in My sight" (Isaiah 43:4). Therefore it is My special delight to educate you.

Are you in money difficulties? Is it hard to make both ends meet? This thing is from Me, for I am your purse-bearer, and would have you draw from and depend upon Me. My supplies are limitless (Philippians 4:19). I would have you prove My promises. Let it not be said of you, "you did not believe the LORD your God" (Deuteronomy 1:32).

Are you in difficult circumstances, surrounded by people who do not understand you, who never consult your taste, who put you in the background? This thing is from Me. I am the God of circumstances. You came not to this place by accident; it is the very place God meant for you. Have you not asked to be made humble? See, then, I have placed you in the very school where this lesson is taught; your surroundings and companions are only working out My will.

Are you passing through a night of sorrow? This thing is from Me.

I am the "Man of Sorrows, and acquainted with grief." I have let earthly comforters fail you, that, by turning to Me, you may obtain everlasting consolation (2 Thessalonians 2:16–17).

Has some friend disappointed you? One to whom you opened your heart? This thing is from Me. I have allowed this disappointment to come, that you may learn.

I want to be your Confidant. Has someone repeated things about you that are untrue? Leave them to Me, and draw closer to Me, thy shelter out of reach of "the strife of tongues," for I "shall bring forth My righteousness as the light, and My judgment as the noonday" (Psalm 37:6).

Have your plans been upset? Are you bowed down and weary?

This thing is from Me. You made your plans, then came asking Me to bless them; but I would have you let Me plan for you, and then I take the responsibility; for "this thing is too much for you, you are not able to perform it by yourself" (Exodus 18:18). You are only an instrument, not an agent.

Have you longed to do some great work for Me, and instead been laid aside on a bed of pain and weakness? This thing is from Me. I could not get your attention in your busy days, and I want to teach you some of My deepest lessons. "They also serve who only stand and wait." Some of My greatest workers are those shut out from active service, that they may learn to wield the weapon of prayer.

Are you suddenly called upon to occupy a difficult

and responsible position? Launch out on Me. I am trusting you with the possession of difficulties. "For this thing the LORD your God will bless you in all your works and in all to which you put your hand" (Deuteronomy 15:10).

This day I place in your hands this pot of holy oil; make use of it freely, My child. Let every circumstance as it arises, every word that pains you, every interruption that would make you impatient, every revelation of your own weakness, be anointed with it! Remember, interruptions are divine instructions. The sting will go as you learn to see Me in all things.

Therefore "set your hearts on all the words which I testify among you today . . . For it is not a futile thing for you, because it is your life, and by this word you shall prolong your days in the land" (Deuteronomy 32:46–47).[4]

The moment we accept the fact that our ordeal has been permitted, even intended, by God, our perspective on disruptive moments will totally change. We will find ourselves saying, "God, You have allowed this in my life. I don't understand it, but I know that it couldn't have happened to me unless it was filtered through Your loving hands. So, this thing is from You."

PRINCIPLE #2: PROGRESS WITHOUT PAIN IS USUALLY NOT POSSIBLE

We live in a skin-deep world. Our culture glorifies clothing, fashion, makeup, tummy tucks, and nose jobs. There may be nothing wrong with any of these, but in the end they are only cosmetic. Character and substance are shaped in the crucible of adversity. Show me someone who lives a carefree life with no problems or trials or dark nights of the soul, and I'll show you a shallow person.

Unless there is pain in the formula, we will never stop to listen carefully to what He is saying. We'll be moving along happily, thinking we're going somewhere—but in reality, we're only spinning our wheels. We're not making any progress at all toward the deeper things our Father longs to show us. Sometimes He must allow us to stumble along the everyday journey. We're wounded and filled with pain, yet our disaster is just the opposite of what it seems; it's the demonstration of God's "tough love"—His determination to teach us and to make us wiser and stronger.

Life, then, brings all of us disruptions. It's up to us to choose our response. It can make us bitter, or it can make us better.

If we choose to let the disruptive moment make us better, we will toughen up. Listen again to Gordon MacDonald:

> The spiritual masters have taught us . . . that the one who would get in touch with his soul must do so with diligence and determination. One must overcome feelings, fatigue, distractions, errant appetites, and popular opinion. One must not be afraid of silence, of stillness, or of entering the overpowering presence of divinity with a humble spirit.[5]

PRINCIPLE #3: THE PROMISE OF GOD IS THE PROVISION OF GRACE

One of the more urgent themes in Scripture is the voice of God saying to us over and over, "My grace is sufficient. My strength is made perfect in weakness. You are My child, and I will deal with you as My child."

I'd like to direct you to one more snapshot from Scripture that completes the picture of God's provision in times of pain. You'll find it in John 15:1–8:

> "I am the true vine, and my Father is the gardener. He cuts off every branch in me that bears no fruit, while every branch that does bear fruit he prunes so that it will be even more fruitful. You are already clean because of the word I have spoken to you. Remain in me, as I also remain in you. No branch can bear fruit by itself; it must remain in the vine. Neither can you bear fruit unless you remain in me.
>
> "I am the vine; you are the branches. If you remain in me and I in you, you will bear much fruit; apart from me you can do nothing. If you do not remain in me, you are like a branch that is thrown away and withers; such branches are picked up, thrown into the fire and burned. If you remain in me and my words remain in you, ask whatever you wish, and it will be done for you. This is to my Father's glory, that you bear much fruit, showing yourselves to be my disciples" (NIV).

In this passage, Jesus borrowed a word picture from the plant kingdom. He explained that because He loves us, He must do some pruning in order for us to thrive and blossom. Do you understand how this principle works in gardening? Even with green things, God's concept of discipline holds true.

But the Gardener is loving and devoted. Warren Wiersbe said, "Your heavenly Father is never nearer to you than when

He is pruning you." That statement is right on the mark. You will find this truth consistently affirmed in the lives of wise, godly people who have faced disruptive moments. They will look at you and say without hesitation, "Never in all my life have I sensed the closeness and provision of God as I did when I came to the bend in the road. Never before have I been more fruitful than I've been since I came through that season when everything seemed upside down."

PRINCIPLE #4: DISRUPTIVE MOMENTS PRODUCE DYNAMIC GROWTH

You can struggle against the disruptive moment, shake your fist at the heavens, and find yourself exhausted, defeated, and in despair—or you can accept the moment and let it train and strengthen you. When you take the latter course, you'll discover on the other side more power, more holiness, and more fruit. Those are precious gifts that cannot be purchased with any coin other than tears. When you possess them, you'll comprehend with joy what God wanted so much for you to experience in your life.

God allows no pain without purpose. Instead, He uses pain to dispense power. Once again, His power can rest upon you only when you've abandoned the idea that you're big enough to go it alone. You're not big enough; you'll never make it without depending utterly upon Him and going in His strength. You're destined to fail without righteousness and holiness. And some pruning must take place, with sharpened shears, to cut away those things that would prevent righteousness and holiness in your life. But how liberated you will be, how free to grow toward the heavens, after that pruning is accomplished!

Every plant, of course, must weather a storm every now and then. Ron Mehl wrote,

> Someone once told me that the times when plants grow the most are not necessarily during the warm, gentle rains or beautiful summer days. In fact, during fierce winds and raging storms come times of the most growth. Botanists tell us that if you were to take a cross-section of the earth during a vicious storm, you could literally observe the roots reaching further down into the soil.[6]

Can you feel it when the heavens open up and the wind and the rains thrash you? Can you feel your roots reaching ever deeper into His loving care?

PRINCIPLE #5: WHAT WE RECEIVE FROM DISRUPTIVE MOMENTS DEPENDS UPON HOW WE RESPOND

Everything God had given me to do was growing and thriving. The size of our church had doubled. The number of listeners to our Turning Point nationwide radio ministry had doubled. The books I had written were finding larger audiences. People were responding to our ministry. All of this was for the glory of God. And then, right in the midst of all these blessings came the disruptive moment. On the face of things, it seemed to make so little sense.

Have you had that kind of experience? Just when you had everything lined up in your life exactly as you wanted things to be, you experienced an unwelcome and unanticipated disaster that spoiled everything. And you asked many questions, all beginning with the word *why*.

"Why this, Lord?" you might ask. "Why now? Why not later? Why not someone else?"

We all ask the "why" questions. They're a natural part of being human. But we can ask better questions—we can ask "what" questions: "What, Lord? What would You have me do? What are You trying to teach me?"

I've faced pain, disappointment, doubt, and despair. In the midst of my trials, I've stopped asking the "why" questions and begun to focus on the "what" questions.

Believe me, you can do the same! Even in the most difficult of circumstances. Even when your entire world has been turned on its head. Even when you feel far too weak and far too tired to reach the finish line. Choose to keep the faith. Receive His strength. Don't give up!

I pray that the words of hope you have found in this book will uplift and comfort you as they have me. And I hope my prayer becomes your prayer too:

Lord, what do You want to teach me to make me a better person? What are Your plans to make me more effective? Lead me and guide me through this process, O Lord. Be my teacher; show me Your ways. And don't let me miss any lesson You've prepared for me.

CONCLUSION

What does it look like to keep the faith? We've seen many examples throughout these pages, and we can find many more in the pages of Scripture. God's Word is filled with famous examples of women and men who fought against their fear, moved beyond discouragement, won the victory against worry, and pressed on to finish the race despite their doubts.

Noah is a powerful example of keeping the faith. So are Abraham and Sarah. And Joshua. And Deborah. And Samuel. And Hannah. And Elijah. And Jeremiah. And Mary. And the disciples, including Peter. And Paul. And many others.

But I want to conclude this journey together by focusing on two biblical characters who are decidedly not famous—not well known. They are two women who had interesting and important roles in their community, yet we rarely hear about them in sermons or in songs. People today don't name their children after these women, although it would be a proper tribute if we did.

Here is their story:

Then the king of Egypt spoke to the Hebrew midwives, of whom the name of one was Shiphrah and the name of the other Puah; and he said, "When you do the duties of a midwife for the Hebrew women, and see them on the birthstools, if it is a son, then you shall kill him; but if it is a daughter, then she shall live." But the midwives feared God, and did not do as the king of Egypt commanded them, but saved the male children alive. So the king of Egypt called for the midwives and said to them, "Why have you done this thing, and saved the male children alive?"

And the midwives said to Pharaoh, "Because the Hebrew women are not like the Egyptian women; for they are lively and give birth before the midwives come to them."

Therefore God dealt well with the midwives, and the people multiplied and grew very mighty. And so it was, because the midwives feared God, that He provided households for them.

—Exodus 1:15–21

If you remember the context of this story, the families of Jacob and his sons had moved from Canaan to Egypt when Joseph was second-in-command of that great nation. The Israelites grew and thrived in that land for centuries. In fact, they become so numerous a people that Pharaoh grew nervous. He viewed the Israelites as a risk to his national security. That is why he ordered the Hebrew midwives to kill male babies at the moment of their birth, and that command made it necessary for those midwives to "choose this day whom they would serve."

Shiphrah and Puah were heroes, no argument there. They risked their lives by defying one of the most powerful rulers in the world, and they did so to save the lives of innocent children.

Yet Shiphrah and Puah were also ordinary people. They were regular women with regular careers who—as Scripture points out on two separate occasions—"feared God." They understood the danger they were in. Pharaoh had the power to end their lives with a word if they displeased him, yet they chose to directly disobey his command because they were motivated by fear of a Higher Power. A higher cause.

It's likely that those midwives attended to Moses' mother when she gave birth to her firstborn son. A "beautiful child" according to Exodus 2:2. Those midwives remained under orders to kill that beautiful boy, but they again refused. They again chose to fear God more than Pharaoh as they helped bring Moses into our world. By doing so, those ordinary midwives with their regular routines and regular jobs paved the way for the exodus from Egypt. They opened the door to the promised land for God's chosen people.

In other words, the midwives helped deliver their people in more ways than one! They played a great role in giving birth to Israel as a nation.

Shiphrah and Puah kept the faith. They did not allow fear or discouragement or worry or doubt to pull them away from what they knew to be right. They put their fate in God's hands, and He rewarded them: "Therefore God dealt well with the midwives" (Exodus 1:2).

But notice, by choosing to stand strong and refusing to take the easy road, those midwives also generated a blessing for their entire community: "Therefore God dealt well with the midwives, and the people multiplied and grew very mighty."

Would you believe you and I have the same opportunity? We do.

You do. Every day. Even with your ordinary job. Even with your ordinary routine. Even with your ordinary place in your ordinary community.

In fact, it's precisely because you and I are ordinary people that we must keep the faith even when our world turns upside down. We must continue pressing forward in the belief that God is with us, that God will empower us, and that God will support us no matter what obstacles we encounter or what threats attempt to bar our way.

When we act from our fear of God rather than fear of the world, we can change that world. We can make a real difference not only in our lives and our communities but in history—as Shiphrah and Puah did.

So be ready! Be willing! Be strong and courageous!

NOTES

FOREWORD

1. Laurel Wamsley, "The Father Who Helped His Son Cross the Finish Line at the Olympics Has Died," NPR, October 4, 2022, www.npr .org/2022/10/04/1126776697/jim-redmond-derek-olympics-sprinter -father-dies.

CHAPTER 1: FIGHT YOUR FEAR

1. This story is adapted from personal correspondence sent by a Turning Point listener.

2. Jerry Adler et al., "The Fight to Conquer Fear," *Newsweek*, 103, no. 17 (April 23, 1984): 69.

3. Adler et al., "The Fight to Conquer Fear."

4. Craig Massey, "When Fear Threatens," *Moody Monthly* 71 (September 1970): 22–23, 69–70.

5. Mark Twain, *Pudd'nhead Wilson and Those Extraordinary Twins* (New York: Penguin Classics, 1986), 138.

6. Joe B. Brown, "Caught in the Grip of Fear," *Moody Monthly* 97, no. 1 (September/October 1996): 11.

CHAPTER 2: DESTROY YOUR DISCOURAGEMENT

1. "Luck Rivals Worst of Sick Jokes: 'There's Hope,' New Yorker Says," *Los Angeles Times*, March 19, 1995, www.latimes.com/archives/la-xpm-1995-03-19-mn-44484-story.html.
2. Johnny Mercer and Harold Arlen, "Ac-Cent-Tchu-Ate The Positive," www.azlyrics.com/lyrics/johnnymercer/accenttchuatethepositive.html.
3. Andy Andrews, ed., "Erma Bombeck," *Storms of Perfection Volume 2* (Nashville, TN: Lightning Crown Publishers, 1994), 51. Cited in John Maxwell's *Failing Forward: Turning Mistakes into Stepping Stones for Success* (Nashville, TN: Thomas Nelson, 2000), 24–25.
4. Leith Anderson, *Leadership That Works: Hope and Direction for Church and Parachurch Leaders in Today's Complex World* (Minneapolis: Bethany Publishing House, 1999), 166–67.
5. Anderson, *Leadership That Works*, 166–67.
6. Fred Smith, "The Gift of Greeting," *Christianity Today* 29, no. 18 (December 13, 1985): 70.

CHAPTER 3: WIN AGAINST WORRY

1. In Dale Carnegie's *How to Stop Worrying and Start Living* (New York: Pocket Books, 1984), 3–4.
2. *Daily Bread*, December 11, 1999.
3. Thomas Tewell, "The Weight of the World [1995]," *Preaching Today*, tape no. 147.
4. Daniel R. Mitchum, "The Needless Burden of Worry," *Discipleship Journal*, March 1, 1987, 44–46.

CHAPTER 4: DISARM YOUR DOUBTS

1. Mark Littleton, "Doubt Can Be Good," *HIS*, March 1979, 9.

CHAPTER 5: THE GIFT OF GRACE

1. Quoted in Lettie Cowman, *Streams in the Desert* (Grand Rapids, MI: Zondervan, 1965), 90.
2. Kenneth Wuest, *Wuest's Word Studies from the Greek New Testament*, vol. 3 (Grand Rapids, MI: Eerdmans, 1973), 82.
3. Paul Lee Tan, *Encyclopedia of 7000 Illustrations: A Treasury of Illustrations, Anecdotes, Facts, and Quotations for Pastors, Teachers, and Christian Workers*, electronic ed. (Garland, TX: Bible Communications, 1979). Published in electronic form by Logos Research Systems, 1997.
4. John Newton, *Out of the Depths*, revised by Dennis R. Hillman (Grand Rapids, MI: Kregel, 2003), 12.
5. Ron Mehl, *Surprise Endings: Ten Good Things About Bad Things* (Sisters, OR: Multnomah, 1993), 60.
6. Quoted in Josiah Bull, *"But Now I See": The Life of John Newton* (Carlisle, PA: Banner of Truth Trust, 1998), 304.
7. Bull, *"But Now I See,"* 304.

CHAPTER 6: THE POWER OF PERSEVERANCE

1. Adapted from David L. Allen, "My All-Time Favorite Sports Sermon Illustration!," March 13, 2019, https://drdavidlallen.com/sermons/my-all-time-favorite-sports-sermon-illustration/; see also Julietta Jameson, *Cliffy: The Cliff Young Story* (Melbourne, Australia: Text Publishing, 2013).
2. See Douglas J. Moo, *The NIV Application Commentary: 2 Peter, Jude* (Grand Rapids, MI: Zondervan, 1996), 46.
3. Eugene Peterson, *A Long Obedience in the Same Direction* (Downers Grove, IL: InterVarsity Press, 2000), 131–32.
4. Adapted from "Byron Janis (Piano)," accessed March 27, 2019, www.bach-cantatas.com/Bio/Janis-Byron.htm.

5. "Byron Janis (Piano)."

6. Dena Yohe, *You Are Not Alone* (New York: WaterBrook, 2016), 12, 121.

7. Chris Tiegreen, *The One Year Walk with God Devotional* (Wheaton, IL: Tyndale House Publishers, Inc., 2004), March 6.

8. Adapted from Omee Thao, "Difficult Journey Leads to Blessed Life," *Alliance*, accessed March 30, 2019, www.cmalliance.org/news /2015/04/09/difficult-journey-leads-to-blessed-life/.

9. Joni Eareckson Tada, *Heaven: Your Real Home* (Grand Rapids, MI: Zondervan, 2018), 171.

10. Gerri Willis, "Breast Cancer Taught Me to Live Day by Day, Hour by Hour," *Good Housekeeping*, October 27, 2017, www.good housekeeping.com/health/a46636/gerri-willis-breast-cancer/.

11. Peter Rosenberger, *Hope for the Caregiver* (Nashville, TN: Worthy Publishing Group, 2014), 99–100.

12. Adapted from Eun Kyung Kim, "Inspiring 3-Year-Old Twins with Down Syndrome Have Become Social Media Stars," *Today*, March 27, 2019, www.today.com/parents/inspiring-3-year-old-twins -down-syndrome-have-become-social-t151064.

13. Anne Lamott, "I am going to be 61 years old in 48 hours," Facebook, April 8, 2015, www.facebook.com/AnneLamott/posts/66217757724 5222.

14. Zoë Read, "Daughter of Fallen Wilmington Firefighter Receives National Scholarship," *WHYY*, February 5, 2019, https://whyy.org /articles/daughter-of-fallen-wilmington-firefighter-receives-national -scholarship/.

15. Helen Wilbers, "Record-Setting Hiker Shares Lesson," *News Tribune*, May 27, 2018, www.newstribune.com/news/local/story/2018/may/27 /learning-on-her-feet/728085/.

16. Stephanie Gallman, "Elite Runner Crawls Across the Finish Line at

Austin Marathon," CNN, February 17, 2015, www.cnn.com/2015/02
/16/us/austin-marathon-finish-line-crawl/index.html.

17. Adam Hammons, "Runners Inspired by Crawl to Finish Line," CBS
Austin, February 17, 2015, https://cbsaustin.com/sports/content
/runners-inspired-by-crawl-to-finish-line.

CHAPTER 7: THE ROLE OF RESPONSIBILITY

1. Phil Helsel, "Kyrie Irving to Donate $500k to Fight Hate, Takes
Responsibility for Post about Antisemitic Film," NBC News,
November 2, 2022, www.nbcnews.com/news/us-news/kyrie-irving
-oppose-forms-hatred-take-responsibility-post-antisemitic-rcna
55380.

2. Quoted in Craig Brian Larson, ed., *750 Engaging Illustrations for
Pastors, Teachers, and Writers* (Grand Rapids, MI: Baker Books,
2002), 40.

3. Julie Juola-Exline, Ann Marie Yali, and Marci Lobel, "When God
Disappoints: Difficulty in Forgiving God and Its Role in Negative
Emotions," *Journal of Health Psychology* 4, no. 3 (1999): 365–79,
https://doi.org/10.1177/135910539900400306.

4. Thomas Schlamme, dir. "Two Cathedrals," *The West Wing,* season
2, episode 22, Warner Bros. Television, 2001.

5. Eva J. Alexander, "Rescuing Women," *Decision*, October 1997, 4–5.

CHAPTER 8: THE FUNDAMENTALS OF FORTITUDE

1. Gordon MacDonald, *The Life God Blesses* (Nashville, TN: Thomas
Nelson, 1994), 25.

2. MacDonald, *The Life God Blesses*, 25.

3. Aleksandr Solzhenitsyn, *The Gulag Archipelago, Vol. 2*, quoted in
Annie Holmquist, "Aleksandr Solzhenitsyn's Advice for a World
Plagued by Chaos and Victimhood," Intellectual Takeout, October 25,

2018, www.intellectualtakeout.org/2018/10/aleksandr-solzhenitsyns
-advice-for-a-world-plagued-by-chaos-and-victimhood/.

4. Laura A. Barter Snow, "This Thing Is from Me," tract 120 (Grand
Rapids, MI: Faith, Prayer, and Tract League), n.d.

5. MacDonald, *The Life God Blesses*, 42.

6. Mehl, *Surprise Endings*, 60.

ABOUT THE AUTHOR

David Jeremiah is the founder of Turning Point, an international ministry committed to providing Christians with sound Bible teaching through radio and television, the internet, live events, resource materials, and books. He is the author of more than fifty books, including *Forward*, *Overcomer*, *A Life Beyond Amazing*, *Airship Genesis: Kids Study Bible*, and *The Jeremiah Study Bible*.

Dr. Jeremiah serves as the senior pastor of Shadow Mountain Community Church in San Diego, California, where he resides with his wife, Donna. They have four grown children and twelve grandchildren. Learn more at DavidJeremiah.org.

Stay Connected to Dr. David Jeremiah

Take advantage of three great ways to let
Dr. Jeremiah give you spiritual direction every day!

Turning Points Magazine & Devotional

Have Dr. David Jeremiah's monthly magazine
delivered directly to your home. Each issue
includes:

- A thematic study focus
- Relevant articles
- Daily devotional readings
- Bible study resource offers
- Radio & television information

Request *Turning Points* magazine today!
(800) 947-1993 | DavidJeremiah.org/Magazine

Daily Turning Point E-Devotional

Find words of inspiration and spiritual
motivation in your inbox every morning.
Each e-devotional from David Jeremiah will
strengthen your walk with God and encourage
you to live with authentic faith.

Sign up for your free e-devotional today!
DavidJeremiah.org/Devo

Turning Point Mobile App

Access Dr. David Jeremiah's video teachings,
audio sermons, and more ... whenever and
wherever you are.

Download the free app today!
DavidJeremiah.org/App